LOLA R.

*The*GOSPELS CHALLENGE

30 Days Through the Words
and Miracles of Jesus

SPIRIT REIGN
PUBLISHING
A Division of Spirit Reign Communications

Cover Design: Daryl Anderson

Interior Page Design & Layout: OA.Blueprints, LLC

Printed in the United States of America

978-1-940002-82-8 (PB)
978-1-940002-83-5 9 (ePDF)
978-1-940002-84-2 (ePUB)

SPIRIT REIGN
PUBLISHING
A Division of Spirit Reign Communications

CONTENTS

LET'S MAKE A PLAN

I wanted to share a few ideas for how to get the most out of this challenge. Of course, none of it is mandatory, but the ideas I share will really help you to maximize the time you invest in this reading over the next month.

1. Create a Habit
Studies have shown that new habits can be formed in as little as twenty-one days. Later studies challenge the short time frame but I'll say this, after thirty days of committing to reading scripture, you're well on your way to developing a daily habit of Bible reading. There are a couple of elements you can add to your time to establish a solid ritual.

- Begin around the same time every day.
- Commit to thirty minutes per session.

These practices enable you to carve out time and space for God on a daily basis.

2. Use a Journal
During the daily readings, the journal will give you a place to jot down words or verses that speak to you as well as your prayers based on what you've read. You can even jot down your thoughts and feelings not connected with the text. The journal is important because it helps you to create the foundation for in-depth study, which will be part of a later challenge.

3. Use S.O.A.P.

We're not talking about your showering ritual, but your scriptural ritual. S.O.A.P. is an acronym for Scripture, Observations, Application, and Prayer. It actually gives you a very basic outline for a short devotional time. As an aside, you always start with prayer...asking God to be present as you read.

Now, you'd begin by reading the segment for the day and during the reading, use your journal to jot down the things that stand out to you about the text (i.e., ideas that really stand out, questions that arise from the text, things that speak directly to your situation). You're making observations about what you've read and thought. After you've made observations, ask the question, "How does this apply to me?" There is no one right answer; you're looking for how the text speaks directly to you. Finally, you spend time in prayer, thanking God for what you've read, talking with Him about it, listening to what He says about it, and asking for strength to apply it.

Finally...

You may ask whether you need to use a physical Bible or if you can use one that's electronic (likely on your phone, computer, tablet, etc.). I have personally enjoyed reading Scripture using both options. A physical Bible allows you to write physical notes and is a great option for those who enjoy handling actual books. An electronic Bible offers additional options such as the ability to quickly jump between passages and to highlight key texts. I've also really enjoyed being able to listen to the text being read to me while driving or exercising. Bottom line, the Bible you use is up to you. Whatever the format... get in the Word!

So, are you ready to get started? I am!

"But as for you, continue in what you have learned and have firmly believed, knowing from whom you learned it and how from childhood you have been acquainted with the sacred writings, which are able to make you wise for salvation through faith in Christ Jesus."
2 Timothy 3:14-15

ARE YOU READY TO FIGHT?

For we wrestle not against flesh and blood, but against principalities, against powers, against the rulers of the darkness of this world, against spiritual wickedness in high places.

-Ephesians 6: 12-13

I know, I could have warned you sooner. I thought it would be a good time to chat about the spiritual aspect of this journey.

The Bible says, "For we are not fighting against flesh-and-blood enemies, but against evil rulers and authorities of the unseen world, against mighty powers in this dark world, and against evil spirits in the heavenly places" (Eph. 6:12). Essentially, we may be going about our daily business, operating as usual, but there is an unseen enemy who takes interest in our activities. We usually call him out when times are particularly difficult or when we encounter painful situations. We aren't as prone to do this when we are overwhelmed with great opportunities that make us happy but are meant to crowd-out time spent in the presence of God. All distraction, whether pleasurable or uncomfortable, is designed by our enemy to steal our focus from what is truly important.

Get ready to be distracted.

The enemy, Satan, has no interest in your reading God's word. Don't be surprised if you find yourself struggling to get out of bed or to

The Gospels Challenge by Lola Moore, M. Div

focus. Thirty minutes will, literally, feel like thirty hours! You will experience obstacles like never before when you commit to this challenge. Your children will have a hard time sleeping and keep you up all night; a computer will crash causing precious files to be lost that will leave you scrambling for answers. Now, I don't want you to just expect bad things. You could hear from a friend or family member you haven't spoken to in years or get a new, exciting opportunity that suddenly claims all your free time. Listen, it doesn't matter what kind of distraction it is, good or bad, it's still a distraction.

Reading God's Word prepares you for supernatural warfare. You open yourself to be led and empowered by the Spirit of God daily, and the enemy does not want that! So, you'll get started and find yourself becoming bored. I'll write a message with typos and because you're turned-off by me, you'll be tempted to stop reading the Word! I'm telling you, it's coming! But you must make a commitment right now! Commit to reading God's Word so that you can equip yourself to do His work. When you prayerfully face the challenge, God will help you to reap the benefits.

Let's schedule an appointment:

The time I will begin reading tomorrow:_____

Where will I read tomorrow? _____

I am so excited to take this journey with you!

INTRODUCTIONS | MATTHEW 1-3

"Look! The virgin will conceive a child! She will give birth to a son, and they will call him Immanuel, which means 'God is with us."

- Matthew 1:23

I realize it may take a bit more time than we're prepared for to present a proper introduction to the book of Matthew. In short, a former tax collector, the Apostle Matthew, wrote Matthew. He is Jewish and has a specific burden to see his kinsmen saved. So Matthew writes in a way that Jewish people can appreciate. His major claim is that Jesus is the promised Messiah and King of Old Testament Prophecy. If you look closely, you'll see that Matthew frequently refers back to what the prophets prophesied concerning the coming Messiah, and how Jesus fulfills all of it.

It's challenging, each time I start reading a book and I see the beginning of a genealogy (Family Tree). But I now see why Matthew takes the time to outline so many of Jesus' ancestors. You should know that Abraham and Moses and David are the most notable figures in Jewish culture. Although Jesus can't be traced back to the line of Moses, see how Matthew ensures that Jesus' family tree clearly links Him to both figures? There will be no doubt in our minds that Jesus is fully connected and qualified to be named the promised Messiah. Understand that all of the stories Matthew will tell are specifically chosen to make this point.

I think about the trouble Matthew went through to get his point across. Remember, he wrote his book after prominent Jewish leaders collaborated to kill Jesus. In fact, the newly-formed Christian church was enduring active persecution by the Jewish leadership. So wait, Matthew is being persecuted by the same people who conspired to kill Jesus, and yet he is still working to provide them with a Gospel that can win them.

He still has a passion to bless those who have been actively imposing hardship on Christianity. Matthew still loves them and wants to share the good news of Jesus with them.

REFLECTIONS

1. Consider the beautiful picture of Jesus painted in these chapters. Would you want to share a "Loving Jesus" or a "Vengeful Jesus" with those who intentionally hurt you?

2. The Jews are feeling oppressed by the Roman government during the time of Jesus and desperately want to be freed. How do you share the truth of a loving and merciful Christ with those who are hurting and abused?

BEGINNINGS
| MATTHEW 4-6

But Jesus told him, No! The Scriptures say,
'People do not live by bread alone but by every word that
comes from the mouth of God.'

- Matthew 4:4

The Bible tells us that "immediately" or "straightway" after Jesus was baptized, He was "driven" by the Holy Spirit into the wilderness to be tempted by the Devil. The word "driven" used here is the same sense or connotation as a person being "driven" to do something after being possessed. So, Jesus didn't have a choice here, He didn't go out as part of a plan to be tempted, the Spirit pressed Him to go; to be tempted by Satan. The next step after Baptism was facing the tempter. Even Jesus didn't get a break between a "high day" and a test.

He goes out and fasts for forty days and nights in the wilderness; no conversation, no food, no water. Jesus spends forty days denying Himself before He meets the enemy. Before Jesus defeats Satan, He defeats Himself! Jesus spends almost six weeks saying "no" to

His personal urges and needs before He faces the enemy. There are honestly some failures we endure, not at the hands of Satan, but at our own two hands. We haven't demanded that our urges and desires obey us. We are somehow the servant to the messages our bodies and minds give us. Jesus teaches us that before we can ever be successful in defeating Satan, we must be successful in defeating ourselves. Whew... on the verge of starvation and deeply suffering dehydration, with cracked lips and exposed ribs, Jesus is now stronger than He's ever been.

On day forty, Satan approaches. He begins his temptation right where Jesus' number one survival essential is, food. Satan says, "If you're the Son of God, go ahead, make these stones into bread." Without food, Jesus would die soon, he needs to eat! However, Jesus declined because He refused to satisfy even His desperate need on His own.

He was committed to depend on God for everything, even the thing He was dying to have! Jesus refused to have anything that didn't come directly from His Father's hand. He would rather die than circumvent the work of God in His life. Mercy! He goes on to deny the security of knowing God would keep His word and the security of bypassing the cross because He trusted the Father that much!

So here it is; Jesus mastered Himself and Satan before He began His public work. He had private mastery before assuming a public ministry. Even Jesus refused to skip steps. Many of us fail because we're trying to battle ourselves and the enemy in our personal lives at the same time as we do public work for others. Even Jesus put first things first.

REFLECTIONS

Jesus lived in a way that demonstrated that the Father could be trusted to provide all the protection and power we could ever need. What keeps you (and me) from trusting when we are in rough situations?

THE NATURE OF THE KINGDOM | MATTHEW 7-9

*"Anyone who listens to my teaching
and follows it is wise, like a person who builds a
house on solid rock."*

- Matthew 7:24

After Jesus emerges from the wilderness, He begins His ministry. The first recorded ministry of Jesus was His preaching ministry. He preached with power. Matthew records His "Sermon on the Mount" and boy, what a sermon it is! Jesus lays out the basic values and nature of the Kingdom of Heaven and they are totally opposed to the nature and value of kingdoms on Earth. Essentially, every knee-jerk human behavior of self-promotion or posturing, Jesus replaces with promoting the kingdom. Protection of self is replaced with protecting others. Jesus teaches that joining the Kingdom means re-evaluating every relationship, every expectation and every value. Jesus says to live for the Kingdom means death to virtually every other deeply held value. Each time I read it, the radical nature of what Jesus is demanding makes me reevaluate my commitment.

Jesus talks about radical forgiveness and radical trust and their absolute necessity for the kingdom citizen. Then, for today's reading, He breaks living in the Kingdom down to the simplest concept: Obedience.

A song I learned as a child sums it up: "The wise man built his house upon a rock and when the rain came down and the flood came up, the house on the rock stood firm! The foolish man built his house upon the sand, but when the rains came down and the floods went up, the house on sand went "SPLAT!""

Houses can't withstand storms unless they are built on a firm foundation and we can't withstand temptation unless our lives are built on Christ. Building on Jesus consists of a few things. Jesus sums them up as hearing His Word and obeying it.

Not eloquent, but pretty accurate. We can look great on the outside, but we will lack true power unless we are anchored in Christ. And Jesus demonstrates that being anchored doesn't mean membership in a religious community or serving in a position but simply obeying the word of God.

Living on beachfront property seems luxurious until a storm hits. It's extravagant to be so close to the water and to observe the waves crashing against the shore, but it all seems idiotic when the storm comes. Then, victims are confronted with their flawed logic. There are no shortcuts when it comes to building a home that will keep you and your family safe. It is only true and radical obedience to God's word that will sustain us during the storms of life.

REFLECTIONS

1. What is the most challenging section of "The Sermon on the Mount" for you?

2. If you've already been building a house on sand, how do you make the transition to building on rock?

THE COST OF DISCIPLESHIP | MATTHEW 10-12

"Are you the Messiah we've been expecting, or should we keep looking for someone else? Jesus told them, "Go back to John and tell him what you have heard and seen– the blind see, the lame walk, the lepers are cured, the deaf hear, the dead are raised to life, and the Good News is being preached to the poor."

- Matthew 11:3-5

During yesterday's reading, Jesus is gathering a great deal of popularity and support because of the miracles He is performing. He continues to preach and He is preaching with an authority the people have never witnessed before. As He goes along, He is attracting "disciples" or devout followers. It is important to notice that there are dozens of disciples around Him and of those disciples, Jesus identifies The Twelve, a select group of followers who Jesus will pour into.

We learn that Jesus anoints these twelve and gives them a level of power that few people possessed in that day. It's interesting to note that Jesus is able to transfer His power to others. This is not a common ability. Most powerful figures seek to reserve the level of power Jesus had for themselves. They want to build their own name and reputation. Jesus doesn't seek to hoard the power for Himself but gives to His disciples the power to heal disease and to cast out demons.

Now there are thirteen people in the region who also have the power to tear down Satan's kingdom. You would assume this is win-win for everyone. Now, there are thirteen different avenues by which sick people can be made whole. Who wouldn't be happy about that? But Jesus quickly tells them that the response to them would often be laden with hatred. Rather than praise and privilege, Jesus assures them that persecution is the reward for those advancing the cause of the Kingdom.

As if on cue, word comes from John the Baptist, who has been imprisoned for his preaching. John has lived a life of self-denial; he's preached faithfully, he is fruitful! Yet he is in prison. I think this is critical, we have to learn and accept that faithfulness is its own reward. We often find ourselves believing that there is some outcome other than the experience of faithfulness that we are entitled to. Jesus says clearly, that is not the case. Faithfulness is its own reward!

We must trust God to provide whatever we truly need and to keep us in whatever lows or valleys that come as a result of being faithful. Again, faithfulness is its own reward.

REFLECTIONS

1. Have you ever experienced blessing others while your personal situation was uncomfortable?

2. Is it "enough" to know that you have been faithful during times where you go through personal hardships?

GOOD SEED...
GOOD GROUND
OF THE KINGDOM
| MATTHEW 13-15

"The seed that fell on good soil represents those who truly hear and understand God's word and produce a harvest of thirty, sixty, or even a hundred times as much as had been planted!"

- Matthew 13:23

"A farmer goes out to sow..." This farmer throws seed everywhere and the seed is good! However, not all of the seed bears fruit. The success of the seed is not a reflection on the seed itself, but on the type of ground it falls onto. Only good ground, ground that is cleared of competing elements, will receive seed and experience wonderful growth.

"The Kingdom is like a farmer who planted good seed in a field..." The farmer rests knowing he was diligent, but when the crop begins to grow, he sees the work of his enemy...among the wheat he's diligently sown, there are weeds! Well-meaning servants see this and want to clean-up the negative elements but the farmer is wise. He knows that to remove all the weeds, they will unwittingly pull out wheat as well. So the farmer makes a decision. To protect the wheat, he'll allow the weeds to keep growing. Although the cleansing won't happen today, with an expert hand, he'll separate the good crop from the weeds himself!

"The Kingdom is like a mustard seed..." barely visible, at first, but with time and the right environment, that mustard seed will blossom into a huge tree that not only bears fruit but is also a habitat for birds to live in.

Looking at these parables, I am invited to catch a glimpse of the heart and mind of God. These seeds are insignificant, at first, but with time and proper attention, they all grow. This is the power of God deposited into the willing heart. That Word has potential to bring about outcomes we'd never dreamt of but the question isn't whether the seed is "potent" but whether our hearts have been cleared of the preoccupations and motives that stifle what the Word can accomplish.

The question I have for myself is, what kind of soil am I presenting to the Savior? Vultures or weeds exist in me that could stifle the Word, in me. How do I know when I'm not good ground? We need to pray that our hearing of these parables doesn't become so familiar that we not take inventory of our own condition. May Jesus do the work of cleaning out these hearts of ours today, is my prayer.

REFLECTIONS

If you find your heart isn't a safe environment for the seed of God's word, how do you change that?

Day 6

SHADOWS OF THE CROSS
| MATTHEW 16-18

"If any man will come after me, let him deny himself, and take up his cross, and follow me. For whosoever will save his life shall lose it: and whosoever will lose his life for my sake shall find it."

- Matthew 16:24-25 KJV

It feels as if we've had an extended introduction to Jesus, His values, and the true foundation of the Kingdom of God over the past few days. We've seen what is truly important to Christ as well as the fundamental characteristics of those who should follow Him. We have seen that no power, whether political or supernatural, could stand against Christ and prevail. We have been reassured that He is the Messiah everyone's been looking for; Jesus is all they prophesied and more! Just when we've gotten used to Him, He talks about leaving.

In a private conversation, it comes out that even though there is some confusion amongst the larger crowds of those following Him, the disciples actually believe that Jesus is "the Christ, the Son of the Living God." Whew, thank goodness...the disciples sometimes don't get it. But after Jesus rejoices that they get it, He reminds them of what the Promised One actually came to do. He lets them know that even though He's successfully dodged the attacks of the religious authorities, they eventually would successfully kill Him. And the same disciple who made the defining declaration regarding Jesus' identity now precedes an attempt at containing him.

Peter believes that because he has a right answer about the Savior, he is now more right than Christ about how His identity plays-out in real time. So now, because Peter has identified Jesus as the Christ, Peter believes he is directing how Jesus will behave and respond.

Isn't it interesting what happens when we become too comfortable with Christ? Our "comfort" traditionally manifests itself in our declarations of what God will and will not do; what is like God and what isn't steed heavily in our selfishness and how we want us and ours to be treated versus them and theirs. And just when our self-righteousness peaks, Jesus chimes in, "Get behind me, Satan." But wait, Jesus! I'm on your side! How did this go so wrong so fast? "You are seeing things merely from a human point of view, not from God's."

Jesus doesn't want us to become too comfortable with His current presence and work. He is never so stuck in the present success of His ministry that He loses sight of what is to come. Our tendency is the desire to duplicate His life, His miracles, His authority and preaching, His power...

But Jesus reminds us that the defining characteristic of His followers is duplicating his death. He says, "If any of you wants to be my follower, you must turn from your selfish ways, take up your cross and follow me." Jesus' ministry culminates with Him making the ultimate sacrifice. He's not preoccupied with what He'll receive, He's focused on what He will give. I think I would be okay with Jesus reserving that expectation for Himself, but He now obliges us to do the same: If you try to hang on to your life, you will lose it, but if you give up your life for my sake, you will find it.

And what do you benefit if you gain the whole world but lose your soul? Is anything worth more than your soul? It's hard enough to live for the Lord; I'm really praying for His strength and spirit to die for Him as well.

REFLECTIONS

1. What ideas or behaviors is God leading you to put to death in your life?

2. When you think of carrying your own cross, does the promise of meeting Jesus personally seem worth it?

THERE IS A FLAG
| MATTHEW 19-21

"Humanly speaking, it is impossible.
But with God everything is possible."

- Matthew 19: 26

There are days I've been tempted to believe I'm a good person. I try to help people where I can, I actually study and present Scripture as an occupation. I'm not mean-natured or dishonest, so I've believed that I'm, at least, not a bad person. But Jesus has an uncanny way of exposing the true nature of my heart and relieving me of any certainty of my own goodness.

The unveiling of His heart had already begun when the young man approached Jesus, asking, "What good deed must I do to have eternal life?" My eyes squint as I can already tell this isn't going to be good. "Why ask me about what is good?" Hint...hint! Man, take the hint! But Jesus continues trying to help the young man out, "There is only One who is good. But to answer your question, if you want to receive eternal life, keep the commandments." My next question, taking the hint, would have been, "Okay, who's the One who is good?" Because

Jesus has already gently told me that I'm not that One. My first take-away, I'm trying so hard to be "good" and I can't. I cannot be what I am not.

So, if you go with me, this conversation is a set-up. This guy wants to do a "good thing" to receive a reward, eternal life. Jesus replies, there's only One who is good; only that One can earn and secure eternal life. End of conversation, right? Wrong, because the young man doesn't get it. He doesn't want to take the "easy" way out. He doesn't need help navigating life, he's able to handle that himself. So Jesus gives him the steps...

"Keep the commandments."

Bingo, the young man has this in the bag! He rubs his hands together in anticipation of being commended by the greatest Rabbi around. He has this in the bag! He's been "keeping the commandments" his whole life! For dramatic effect and a glimmer in his eye, he asks, "Which ones?"

"Well," Jesus responds. "Don't murder anyone, don't commit adultery, don't lie, honor your parents and love your neighbor as yourself."

The young ruler prepares himself for the most epic pat on the head in history and, as he prepares for that pat, he's going to get a kick in the pants. A brief review of those commandments reminds me that the first is having no other gods "before God," essentially, not worshipping anyone or anything other than God.

The third commandment is we are not to take the name of the Lord in vain or claim an association with God that isn't honest. The young man's question indicates he has some issues with these two commandments. He may not have any idols hidden in his closets, but each time he passes a mirror, his heart bows down in worship. He is naming God as his Lord when the true love of his life is the man in the mirror. He is so wonderful in his own eyes, he doesn't recognize how poor a state he's in. He is so blinded by self-righteousness, he doesn't understand the absurdity of his query. Remember the "leaven" of the Scribes and Pharisees from yesterday's reading (Matthew. 16:6)? This is the finished product; people offer themselves as examples of righteousness because of their deeds, not knowing those good deeds are like old oil rags in the back of a garage.

Thankfully, Jesus looks on him with compassion as well. Grace covers us even when we are obnoxious. Jesus loves him still. As an indication of that love, Jesus performs open heart surgery right there, without anesthesia or a scalpel.

"What else must I do?"

"Well, you'll be perfect if you sell all you have, give the money to the poor and follow me."

Silence... mouth drops open ...breathing stops ...slow blink.

We can get hung-up on the "selling all" part. We think Jesus was telling us that having riches is a hindrance to following Him. Well, Jesus actually does say that a few verses down. Sorry, I tried to help.

I want to point to a deeper truth that doesn't let those of us with less material possessions off the hook. The commandments are a list of required practices that condition the heart for submission to God. They are a primer for that type of relationship. So, the natural result of keeping them is supposed to be a person who is submissive to God. The commandments aren't an end unto themselves, they are a road leading to submission to God. So, the kicker is, had this young man been keeping the commandments as he believed, any command from Jesus, though painful, would have been carried out because the objective, submission to Christ, had been accomplished in his life (run-on sentence with a lot of commas, but I want you to get it). The end result of commandment keeping isn't boldly standing to declare that a check-list has been completed but humility in God's presence that asks, "What more can I do, Daddy? How can I better serve You today?"

Our goal isn't to plant our flag on the hill of righteousness as if we've conquered it. Perfection comes when God can plant His flag on the hill of our hearts, because He has conquered us. So if it means selling all, or becoming a missionary, or hardest of all, staying quiet and standing still, we will do that because of our surrender and submission to the One who has conquered us (Help us, Lord!).

In that moment, it was all clear. The rich young ruler is shocked, then sad. He wasn't ready. So he turns slowly and leaves. Life isn't as he thought it was. He isn't who he thought he was.

Remember, the goal isn't checking boxes. It isn't brownie points or bragging rights. The goal is a heart that is submitted to God in such a way that anything He commands is as good as done. We can't do that ourselves, we must utterly depend on the One who has conquered us, the One who is good, to now accomplish His good work inside and through us.

REFLECTIONS

1. What are the areas where your loyalty to God's Kingdom is in jeopardy?

2. How does God alert you that your loyalty is in question?

_____

_____

_____

_____

_____

_____

_____

_____

_____

_____

_____

_____

_____

_____

The Gospels Challenge by Lola Moore, M. Div

IN THE MEANTIME
| MATTHEW 22-25

"What sorrow awaits you teachers of religious law and you Pharisees. Hypocrites! For you shut the door of the Kingdom of Heaven in people's faces. You won't go in yourselves and you won't let others enter either."

- Matthew 23:13

"What sorrow awaits you teachers of religious law and you Pharisees. Hypocrites! For you are careful to tithe even the tiniest income from your herb gardens, but you ignore the more important aspects of the law— justice, mercy, and faith. You should tithe, yes, but don't ignore the more important things."

- Matthew 23:23

Jesus has been welcomed into Jerusalem by a waiting crowd in what we call "The Triumphal Entry." He's now operating in the headquarters for the Jewish religion and is becoming bolder every moment about His authority as Messiah and King. We also know this is the last week of His life, before the cross, so He is working desperately to ensure His disciples understand who He really is. As Jesus becomes bolder, the Pharisees and Sadducees become more desperate to see Him destroyed.

Although Jesus ensures they know who He really is, He also takes a good amount of time sharing information about the time of the end with them. Our minds traditionally venture toward the book of Revelation where Jesus reveals to John, the Revelator, information regarding the time of the end, but Jesus' discourse actually begins right here. Jesus wants to ensure His followers are thoroughly prepared. He tells them about signs that will occur in nature and in culture that will signal for them the beginning of the end. But notice how Jesus' focus isn't on the events. He points them out, they are clear, but over and over again, He drops parables in to speak not about the inner workings of the government but the inner workings of their hearts.

Jesus tells of the king desperately wanting to invite his subjects to the wedding of his son. But when his servants go out to share the good news, they are abused and killed by those who are supposed to be part of his kingdom. He tells of the unfaithful servant, one who is abusive to his fellow servants when he's supposed to be leading and caring for them in his master's absence. He tells of ten bridesmaids awaiting a wedding they were invited to participate in, but only half of them had the foresight to adequately prepare for the wait by bringing sufficient fuel for the task. Jesus knows that if they haven't prepared their hearts, it won't matter if they can track the occurrences around them. Jesus is concerned not only that His servants will be able to discern the times but that they'll also be able to discern their own hearts.

Our tendency, as humans, is to focus on the sensational. We are enthralled by the talk of shadow-governments and persecution, but Jesus calls our attention to the work we are to prioritize during the time. It is the work of advancing the Kingdom in small, sometimes imperceptible, ways. It is the way of investigating our hearts to ensure that the dark and un-surrendered crevices come to light. It is doing what we can where we are while "keeping time" for the newspaper headlines.

Jesus outlines the events that are to come, but only as a backdrop to the real work of preparation and Kingdom building that should be our real focus. Let's stay aware of the time, but let's also remain diligent so when time is up, we'll be ready.

REFLECTIONS

Pray and ask God what you and the Holy Spirit need to do in preparation for His Coming.

_____

_____

_____

_____

_____

_____

_____

_____

_____

_____

_____

_____

_____

THE MOST WONDERFUL SACRIFICE | MATTHEW 26-28

*"He went on a little farther and bowed with his face
to the ground, praying. 'My Father! If it is possible, let this cup
of suffering be taken away from me. Yet I want your will
to be done, not mine.' "*

- Matthew 26:39

My least favorite part of each of the Gospels is that after such a beautiful and compelling story of Jesus' life and ministry, we arrive at the place where the promised Messiah becomes the crucified Savior.

I find myself at a loss for words because there is so much to highlight. I am first reminded that the death of Jesus not only atones for my life but also reveals the true darkness and evil of sin. Imagine, Jesus, who has been healing, feeding, encouraging and enlightening the people, becomes the target of a murderous plot. They put a hit out on Jesus?! How?! I've been jealous before, I've been insecure, but at some point, I have to tell myself that I'm "tripping"/"bugging"/ taking this thing too far and I have to get a hold of myself. These men don't have that kind of restraint. It's what sin does, it calls for the blood of those who pose a threat to our position and pride.

Jesus' record is so clean that his enemies, the Scribes and Pharisees, concocted lies to assemble a foundation for their charges. The guardians of the truth find their refuge in lies. How ironic. Sin will convince us that our desires are so urgent that compromise is the only way to achieve success. During the holiest week of the Jewish calendar, these men miss all of the invitations to consider the Passover and the lamb's blood shed because of their desire to shed the blood of their enemy.

As we read through the account, the list of Jesus' supporters becomes shorter with each passing verse. We see Judas, filled with the Holy Spirit, yet voluntarily trades God's Spirit for that of the enemy. Peter, who sincerely desires to follow Christ and to stand by Him in the darkest of moments will soon allow fear and uncertainty to chase him away from his post. The other disciples seemingly follow suit and scatter from His side as Calvary nears. Who will stand with Him? Who will boldly claim Him, even at the threat of death? I wonder if Jesus has these questions.

I can imagine He wore that weight in Gethsemane. He returns as it were, to the wilderness. This time, it is not without food and water, but a wilderness of support. Jesus has to face Satan alone, all over again. He prays a number of prayers that night. Most of them are not recorded. We only know of the stress and sincerity He felt. We know that He lay hold to the gates of heaven and had an audience with His Father. What an exchange that must have been. Prayers of protection perhaps. Prayers for His weakened disciples. Prayers for

His family. Prayers concerning the coming tribulation. Prayers for strength. And then, a prayer of surrender.

"My Father! If it is possible, let this cup of suffering be taken away from me. Yet, I want your will to be done, not mine." Surrender.

I can't tell you that I would have made it through Gethsemane. I may have found myself looking for an escape route or trying to negotiate with the Jewish leadership. I would have tried to find as painless a solution as possible. Most of all, I would have tried to find someone to stand with me. But Jesus, He surrendered whatever He was feeling to His Father and made His hopes and desires for the next twenty-four hours subordinate to the will of the Father. It is clear that Jesus did not want to go to the cross. It is also clear that if faithfulness to His Father meant the cross, He was determined to see it through.

The Holy Spirit was able to empower Christ because surrender kept a channel of communication open between them. Though Jesus was afraid, surrender opened the windows and doors of His heart to the work of the Spirit so that the mission would be successful. It was His submission to God that enabled God to help Him. Not help Him to escape...but help Him to stay.

I'm not a great swimmer so the work of lifeguards is of much interest to me. I've heard it said that a lifeguard places themselves in danger when they try to rescue a struggling victim. The kicking and flailing can cause them to take the lifeguard down right along with them. It's that violent struggle to save their own life that makes them impossible to rescue. The struggle doesn't serve to bring them closer to safety. It only prolongs their agony. But the mind of the drowning victim tells them there is something they can do to save themselves. They continue to struggle out of fear, although they don't possess the power or skill to save themselves. So, the lifeguard watches and waits while the swimmer struggles. They stay a safe distance until the swimmer tires out or gives up fighting. It is then that the guard can carry the now compliant swimmer to safety. Perhaps Jesus found Himself flailing in the sea of inevitability. He knew what needed to happen but His nerves were tormenting Him. Of course, Satan whispered in His ear, introducing questions and doubt. He was drenched with sweat and likely exhausted and at the end of it all, we see Jesus stop struggling. He surrenders to His Father, surrenders to the process, and the Holy Spirit emboldens Him to face the cross. What a beautiful picture. To see Jesus relax and the Holy Spirit carry Him through false accusations and a Kangaroo court. Jesus relaxes and the Spirit guides Him through the torture and flogging. Jesus relaxes and the Spirit gives Him strength to walk the "Via dolorosa." Jesus relaxes and the Spirit covers Him in the pain of being nailed to a cross. Jesus relaxes and the Spirit fills Him as His wounds bleed. Jesus relaxes and the Spirit comforts Him as He hands His Father His life. Jesus relaxed and the Spirit kept Him as He closed His eyes in death.

Just wow... I'm trying to write more...but I just... wow.

He surrendered to the Father as our substitute and our pilot case. Jesus is proof positive that surrender to the Father is a safe investment. He demonstrates that giving up our need for control and answers and yielding to the leadership of God, even in the worst of scenarios, is the wisest decision we can ever make. And because Jesus successfully finished his mission, He can now safely guide us to safety, when we surrender to Him.

REFLECTIONS

1. In what areas of your life do you need to give up struggling?

2. What practices can we incorporate now to help us surrender in crisis moments?

JESUS, THE MAN! | MARK 1-3

"Jesus replied, 'Who is my mother? Who are my brothers?' Then he looked at those around him and said, 'Look, these are my mother and brothers. Anyone who does God's will is my brother and sister and mother.'"

- Mark 3:33-35

As I mentioned in the beginning, each Gospel is different and is designed to appeal to a different group of people. Matthew's gospel was tailored to his Jewish family and he was careful to depict Jesus as the promised Messiah and King. Mark is totally different. He is writing to appeal to the Romans of His day. If you think back to the movie Gladiator, you'll remember that Romans see themselves as invincible. They are the current ruling government of the world and any type of weakness is detestable to them. They are arrogant and will dismiss anything they perceive as beneath them. They need to know what Jesus is working with. What can he do? They are not going to follow Jesus if, at any moment, they perceive him as weaker than themselves. So in Mark, Jesus is a superhero! Seriously! Jesus wastes no time. The word "immediately" is used a lot to show that Jesus was a man of action. Notice, Mark doesn't even take time to tell of Jesus' birth story? As I heard Dr. Russell Seay say once of the Romans, "They ain't got time for no babies!" A fact to note is that Mark is believed to have been the first Gospel written. It is much shorter than the others and contains the same relative sequence of events as Matthew and Luke. It is believed that after Mark wrote his Gospel, Matthew and Luke used his as a foundation and filled in details; Matthew from his memory, Luke from interviews and eyewitness accounts.

Spoiler Alert: Mark is not an apostle. (All our road trip battles of "Going to Heaven" have been ruined!) He was not one of the disciples. Mark is a young assistant to Paul and receives his story from what Paul recounted. Although we have come to call it "The Gospel of Mark," it is actually "The Gospel of Paul." It was Paul who started the ball rolling with documenting the story of Jesus. This makes a great deal of sense because remember, the majority of Christ's disciples were not formally educated. Though neither Paul nor Mark were actually present for an up close and personal look at Jesus' ministry, we believe their account is pretty accurate as Matthew makes few changes to the account regarding structure, save the elements that will make it more effective to reach his Jewish readers. Now we can see why the Gospel is so basic. This Gospel is not meant to be thorough, it's meant to be effective.

With all of that in mind, this Gospel springboards directly into Jesus' ministry. He, seemingly, comes from nowhere and takes the region by storm. As He is doing all of this successfully, Mark adds a small glimpse of Jesus' family situation.

"When his family heard what was happening, they tried to take him away. 'He's out of his mind,' they said." Mark 3:21

It is amazing to see what well-meaning people will do. Jesus is actually successfully carrying out His mission in the world and the people closest to Him feel compelled to protect Him from Himself. We have the benefit of Matthew to put flesh around the scenario. Mary and Joseph had been told who Jesus was and what His work was to be, but after 30 years, the mission had become blurry. So, Jesus' family (Mother and younger brothers) come to rescue their brother who had "obviously" lost His mind.

The very brief lesson Jesus taught me today is not depending on those closest to me more than I rely on the God who created me. In a culture where family association essentially made an individual great or undesirable, Jesus has to cut ties altogether and re-define "family." His primary allegiance was not to those who shared His DNA but those who shared His mission and purpose. Any other connection was subject to be terminated, should it interfere with the work Jesus was called to do. Though the speed and tenor of this Gospel have changed, one thing has not. Jesus has to be comfortable walking alone.

What connection do you rely on today? Do you find yourself struggling to balance your "new life" with your "old ties?" Even Jesus had to let go of some people to stay on task.

REFLECTIONS

1. How does your reading of this Gospel feel different than our time in Matthew?

2. How have you assessed your relationships to see if they would work with your life's calling?

Day 11

EAT WHAT YOU HAVE FIRST | MARK 4-6

"Then He added, 'Pay close attention to what you hear. The closer you listen, the more understanding you will be given and you will receive even more.

To those who listen to my teaching, more understanding will be given. But for those who are not listening, even what little understanding they have will be taken away from them.'"

- Mark 4:24, 25

My sisters and I grew up in a not-so-silent competition to ensure no one received anything more than we did. We are all around the same age so the three of us vied for position constantly when it came to getting as much as we could. The setting for said competitions was often around our mother's table. Mom would make her famous-to-us baked macaroni and cheese, which would signal us to take our places. She was wise to insist she serve us, lest our precious treasure find itself on the floor. As you know, competing in any field requires a level of technique. One couldn't haphazardly find themselves in "the winner's circle" unless they had been intentional in jockeying for the position over their opponents. I learned one technique, which was not to wait until my plate was clean to ask for another serving. I would gauge my plate's status constantly and when I had cleaned about 80% of my plate, I would begin to ask for more. I can tell you that, on more than one occasion, I found out the hard way that consuming 80% of my plate also meant filling 80% of my stomach. I have, more than once, found myself on the business-end of an extra serving I had requested but could not consume. So, my mother learned to tune out our requests for more and to monitor the contents of our plates. We lacked the ability to truly calculate the capacity of our stomachs. We paid less attention to that than our glee in knowing there was more food available. So my mother insisted that we finish what we had already been given, so we didn't waste what could be shared with others who were actually hungry because of our greed.

Jesus is teaching in a way that these crowds have never heard before. With authority, He breaks down scripture and concepts into understandable language and with a passion that confirmed He was intimately acquainted with the author. The crowds have gathered time and time again to hear such elocution from a man they knew to be "self-taught. They were wowed and amazed at His teaching and wanted more, much more. Jesus, knowing this, began to monitor their "plates."

The people had heard enough of His teaching to make adjustments to their lives; they were equipped to make changes. But too many of the people were collectors of new ideas but not practitioners of what they'd heard. Understand that collecting ideas was not new. There were many people in Roman culture, Scribes and Pharisees included, who loved to memorize passages and train in public speaking so they could wow crowds by the information they amassed. Rhetoric and debate were not foreign practices. The people were familiar with listening to teachers to be wowed. But Jesus places a higher obligation upon them. They mustn't be collectors of ideas, they needed to actually practice what they'd heard.

Jesus likens His word to light; functional, necessary and metaphorical so that a people living about 2,000 years before Thomas Edison's light bulb could understand. "No one lights a lamp to be placed under a basket or a bed." Illumination is meant, rather, to be a blessing to the entire house. You don't hide it, you put it in a prominent place, like a lamp stand, so that it is of actual use to your home. You light lamps to use them. And so it is with understanding the Word of God. Rather than collecting information for the purpose of discussion and debate, hearing the Word of God is intended to actually teach us how to live.

I think Jesus and my mom may have had a few conversations because these words are very familiar. Jesus says, "Take heed what you hear. With the same measure you use it, it will be measured to you." Whatever you use will determine how much more you will receive. "And to you who hear, more will be given to you." Now understand that hearing, in Hebrew thought, was measured by behavior. So, if I give you information and you heard what I relayed, you'd demonstrate it by doing what I have asked or commanded. If my command or information was not obeyed, then the conclusion would be that I wasn't heard. In Jewish culture, you can't say that you heard something when you haven't obeyed it. So, Jesus gives us an incentive. You will receive more understanding when you live according to what you've already heard.

The Gospels Challenge by Lola Moore, M. Div

"Eat what you have first."

So many of us are looking for new information and concepts when we haven't practiced the information we already have available to us. We love going to seminars and collecting books when there are scores of seminars we have already attended and books we have purchased that have gone untouched. So Jesus lets us know that we will only gain new understanding at the rate that we put the understandings we have already received in practice.

REFLECTIONS

1. Recall three new and exciting things you've learned this calendar year. How many of those concepts are part of the way you currently live?

2. How can you implement just one new practice a week based upon your daily readings?

WHAT DO YOU MEAN, 'IF'?
| MARK 7-9

"How long has this been happening?" Jesus asked the boy's father. He replied, "Since he was a little boy. The spirit often throws him into the fire or into water, trying to kill him. Have mercy on us and help us, if you can."

"What do you mean, 'If I can?' " Jesus asked. "Anything is possible if a person believes."

The father instantly cried out, "I do believe, but help me overcome my unbelief!"

- Mark 9:21-24

Belief is tricky. It can feel silly to believe that a situation that has been one way for as long as you can remember will, in an instant, be changed... permanently. It almost sounds crazy to believe that anything can turn a corner that quickly. We are habitual; it seems most things in nature are that way. Once a reality has developed a pattern, things pretty much stay that way. Right?

Jesus encounters a man who had watched his son suffer for years at the hands of a very violent demon. Rather than playing and laughter, this boy had been unable to even speak because the spirit had made him mute and virtually unresponsive. Without warning, the boy would be thrown to the ground in convulsions and tossed about like a doll. The man heard about Jesus' ability to free people from demonic possession and thought, "Perhaps he can heal my boy, too." The man had a glimmer of hope. He had seen the healing himself. Neighbors who were once crippled or deathly-ill now lived as though the illness had never existed. So the man took a chance to find out whether Jesus could be a blessing to his son as well.

This father traveled with his son to find the area where Jesus would be teaching. They arrive and find the disciples mingling with the people. Maybe he won't even need to bother the Rabbi. The disciples have freed people from demonic possession before. He would ask them and see if they could do something for him. The Bible says that the disciples gave their best attempts but were unable to change the boy's condition. This is unexpected. All of the stories he's heard about Jesus have said that healing happens immediately.

Perhaps the stories aren't true. Well, they must have been true because he'd seen the difference Jesus had made in the lives of people for himself. Maybe his problem was just too big for this Jesus.

Have you ever found yourself wondering if your situation is the exception? Even though you've seen prayer or fasting work for another person's situation, when you tried it, your results weren't the same. Have you ever believed with all the strength you could muster, yet nothing changed? It's already difficult to believe that God can fix a situation on the first try. It's even more challenging to believe after we've tried a time or two and nothing has changed.

Jesus shows up to the scene and the man is trying his best to be respectful. Jesus assesses the situation. What is all the commotion? After seeing the religious leaders and disciples fall over themselves trying to explain, the man realized that he needs to say something for himself. He tells Jesus of his son's plight. He tells Jesus the torment his son has endured over the years and, finally, that he tried to address it by going to Jesus' disciples but nothing happened.

And now, the man makes a request and a challenge of sorts. "Please have mercy upon us and help us, if you can." The gentleman has made a request, but again, Jesus has laid a heart bare. The man has requested a miracle on behalf of his son while letting Jesus "off the hook" if the situation is too difficult for Him. He feels he is doing Jesus a favor, but Jesus sees it as an insult. This man has introduced doubt to a situation where doubt seemed reasonable.

Although the man's experience made doubt probable, Jesus demonstrates that the information provided by our experience has no bearing on what He is able, or willing, to do.

"What do you mean, if?"

Our situations can cause us to judge the power and character of God based purely upon our experience. We must remember that our story is not a measure of God's ability. Our lives, though incredibly concrete for us, are in no way a commentary on the nature and power of God. With just a few words, Jesus reminds this man that what his son has experienced is not who God is. His malady is merely a context in which God can reveal His true nature.

Could Jesus be perched over you as you pray, asking, "What do you mean, 'if'? How can you question if I love you? If I care? If I'm willing? I am willing! I am able! I do care!"

What if we took the "if" out of our prayers? What if we stopped placing contingencies on our requests? Perhaps it's time to keep God on the hook. The book of Hebrews tells us, "So let us come boldly to the throne of our gracious God. There we will receive His mercy, and we will find grace to help us when we need it most." *Hebrews 4:16.* We already know that God can. Let's believe God, without reservation; there are no "ifs" with God.

REFLECTIONS

1. What have you been waiting to receive from God?

2. How do we navigate the space between needing an answer from God and the time when that answer becomes evident?

STOLEN MOMENTS | MARK 10-12

"Then they reached Jericho, and as Jesus and his disciples left town, a large crowd followed Him. A blind beggar named Bartimaeus (son of Timaeus) was sitting beside the road. When Bartimaeus heard that Jesus of Nazareth was nearby, he began to shout, 'Jesus, Son of David, have mercy on me!' 'Be quiet!' many of the people yelled at him. But he only shouted louder, 'Son of David, have mercy on me!' When Jesus heard him, he stopped and said, 'Tell him to come here.' So they called the blind man. 'Cheer up,' they said. 'Come on, he's calling you!' So Bartimaeus threw aside his coat, jumped up, and came to Jesus. 'What do you want me to do for you?' Jesus asked. 'My Rabbi,' the blind man said, 'I want to see!' And Jesus said to him, 'Go, for your faith has healed you.' Instantly, the man could see, and he followed Jesus down the road."

- Mark 10:46-52

I was about ten years old when my favorite Gospel artist, Pastor John P. Kee and the New Life Community Choir, came to my hometown for an open air concert. I knew the protocol; "Make sure you stay with the family and make sure we can see you." I listened to the instructions my parents gave and was well aware of the consequences of deviation but as soon as my feet hit the park where that concert was being held, I took off running. I laid my eyes on the soundstage and determined that I would get a spot right in front of it. I weaved through other concert goers as fast as I could and, eventually, sat right up in front of the spot where Pastor Kee was singing. For a few moments, and risking a good whipping and tongue lashing, I was in Heaven. That was one of the greatest experiences I have ever had and I am fully aware that the experience was mine because I dared to disobey for a greater joy. I can only boast of the experience because the goal set before me was greater than the fear of the punishment that likely awaited me. I knew what I wanted.

So did Bartimaeus.

He had been blind and navigating life as best he could. His livelihood was collecting donations from those passing by to pay for his basic needs. I'm not sure how Bartimaeus heard of Jesus. Maybe he stumbled upon a conversation...or an old friend who once begged with him told of his own encounter with Jesus. Perhaps one of the "regulars" didn't need to beg any longer because he had been healed by Jesus. Somehow, Bartimaeus found out what Jesus could do.

Jesus happened to be passing by one day. Bartimaeus heard of it and knew he had one shot. And the Bible tells us that Bartimaeus cared not who heard him or whoever was upset by his ruckus. Bartimaeus screamed at the top of his lungs, "Have mercy on me!" How undignified. The crowd is trying to move along. Jesus' "handlers" are trying to settle Bartimaeus down but he shouts, the Bible says, "...all the more!" "Have mercy on me!" Have you ever been desperate?

American society gives desperation a really bad name. A desperate person is seen as one who will abandon dignity and make a fool of themselves to achieve a particular outcome. Desperation is looked upon negatively because our unspoken expectation is that dignity should never be abandoned. You should never want anything so badly. One should always be able to keep themselves together. But some things warrant our desperation... don't they? Aren't there some things that we should be willing to sacrifice the opinions of others for? Aren't there some goals and outcomes worth embarrassing ourselves for? There are some blessings and miracles reserved for desperate people. Are you desperate? The Bible says the crowd tried to tell Bartimaeus to get a hold of himself. They told Bartimaeus to hush. He was messing up their nice day with his antics.

They wanted to hear what Jesus was saying and Bartimaeus was making it difficult for them to hear. If he would be quiet, they could learn something new. They rolled their eyes at him and explained to him how refined people behave, but the more they coached, the louder he cried, "Have mercy on me!" Isn't it funny how others become annoyed with your pursuit? How people try to set a boundary on how determined you should be about a goal you've set? Or when you've taken your pursuit of said goal too far? People will talk you out of many a blessing, trying to keep you refined. But Jesus heard him.

Somehow, Jesus' ear is tuned to desperation. While it is a turn-off to mere men, Jesus sees our desperation as a signal to do something special. So Jesus calls Bartimaeus to him. Notice this, Jesus can see... why would Jesus call a blind man to make his way to him? Why would Jesus not take the walk over to the blind man? Bartimaeus is going to have to find his way up from his seated position and to either find someone to help him get to Jesus or fumble through the crowd to follow Jesus' voice. Lastly, it's one thing to talk about desperation, it's quite another to show you are willing to do whatever it takes to see a need filled. Jesus puts Bartimaeus to the test right there. What are you willing to go through to have God meet your need?

Bartimaeus gets to Jesus and is clear with his request. "I want to see!" And because of his persistence, Jesus responds, "Your faith has healed you!"

REFLECTIONS

1. What is one seemingly impossible thing that you need God to do?

2. What are the elements or people that try to convince you to stop asking for what you actually need?

NOT JUST YET
| MARK 13-16

"After Jesus rose from the dead early on Sunday morning, the first person who saw him was Mary Magdalene, the woman from whom he had cast out seven demons. She went to the disciples, who were grieving and weeping, and told them what had happened. But when she told them that Jesus was alive and she had seen him, they didn't believe her."

- Mark 16:9-11

Mary and a group of women have been grieving the murder of their beloved Jesus all Sabbath. They decide to "do something" as women will often do. Jesus hasn't been buried properly so as soon as the Sabbath is over, they set out for Jesus' tomb where He was hurriedly deposited on Friday afternoon. Mary has anointed Him once in life; she will now anoint Him again, in death. They make it to the tomb but something is not right. They had worked it out. Moving the stone would be difficult but they'd explain to the soldiers guarding the tomb that they only wanted to complete the burial process for their friend. Certainly these men would help them. And as they figure out their pitch for help, they realize the stone has already been moved. Not just half way, but the stone is now laying on its side and someone is sitting on it. What in the world is this? The ladies look at each other and try to understand what has happened here. Is this some sort of sick joke? But as they move closer to the figure sitting on their friend's stone, they realize this is not a man...well, it's not a woman, either...this is, an angel? This is not possible! The women look at one another, wondering what is going on. They see the bodies of the men who were supposed to be guarding Jesus' tomb laying on the ground. What is happening here? So the angel speaks. "Don't be afraid." Don't be afraid? How could they be anything but afraid? There's an angel sitting on a stone that is supposed to be sealing Jesus' grave. But somehow, there are bodies on the ground and an angel sitting on the stone. So if all of that is happening outside the tomb...what in the world is going on inside the tomb?

"He's not here."

"Not here?"

"Wait, what do you mean, He's not here? Where have they taken Him? He doesn't have proper clothing on. We only did a patch job because everything happened so fast. Joseph had this tomb and thought about it at the last minute. We have all these spices to anoint Him. If someone would have just told us, we could have made sure He was prepared. Just tell us where He is so that we can prepare Him properly."

"He is alive."

Alive?

Their entire world is rocked! They had heard Jesus say something about being raised after He was killed, but that was ludicrous, right? I mean, who lives after dying? So the women had heard Jesus say it, but didn't truly believe it. Now they are confronted with an ending that is better than they expected.

I wonder if God has a better ending to our sorrows and losses than we expected. We know what should happen at the end of cancer. We know what happens at the end of the argument... at the end of flunking out of school. And many times, we are grieving and preparing spices to get closure and to bury stuff that God has not yet ordained to be dead. We are grieving, we are heart broken, but this situation will not end in death.

These women wasted their time, money and tears because they had counted someone dead who Jesus told them would yet live again. How many things are we counting as dead? Our children who have decided to try life on their own for a time? The possibility of a happy life? A church that is a joy to attend and serve in? We are walking with burial spices and shrouds when Jesus has made promises that they will live again. The women hear the message, drop their preparations, and take off running to tell the disciples, who were also grieving, He is alive! What a wonderful moment when Jesus turns our funeral processions into holiday parades! But how much more wonderful is it when we can see a circumstance in a grave, and because of God's word, we are waiting at the entrance with party poppers, confetti, and kazoos because we know the resurrection is coming. I want faith like that.

REFLECTIONS

1. What have you found yourself trying to bury when God has in-dicated that thing can, and will, live?

2. What makes us ignore God's words of restoration in dying situ-ations?

OFF DAY

And He said to them, "Come aside by yourselves to a deserted place and rest a while." For there were many coming and going and they did not even have time to eat.

- Matthew 6:31

REFLECTIONS

1. What have you learned about Jesus that you didn't know?

2. How has your understanding of scripture grown?

THE UPSIDE-DOWN WAY
| LUKE 1-3

"Many people have set out to write accounts about the events that have been fulfilled among us. They used the eyewitness reports circulating among us from the early disciples. Having carefully investigated everything from the beginning, I also have decided to write a careful account for you, most honorable Theophilus, so you can be certain of the truth of everything you were taught."

- Luke 1:1-3

We have seen two very unique perspectives on the ministry of Jesus. Not only is the personal experiences of Matthew and Mark (who were scribes for Paul) very different, but the audiences they are writing to reach are also very different. As a result, we have seen a change in emphasis and noticed what they have omitted. Luke now presents an even more diverse view of Jesus' life story. Luke is termed "the upside-down Gospel." As you can see, Luke is written to "Theophilus" who seems to have been a new believer. Because of the name used, we're not certain whether Theophilus is an individual or if this is a Gospel written to all new believers. The name Theophilus (Theo=God, Phile=lover), leaves room for either one to be true. Luke's methodology is different as well. We see that Luke has conducted interviews with people who had personally witnessed the ministry of Jesus. Luke is also not an apostle of Jesus. He has learned of, and accepted, the good news of Jesus and is writing this Gospel to strengthen the faith of someone who also is learning of Jesus after His ministry. Luke's background is in medicine, so it is not surprising that he comes to us from a researched perspective.

You will notice that Matthew and Mark were careful to write in a way that is not offensive to those to whom they are addressing. The readers Luke emphasizes do not have either set of hang-ups. So Luke includes major characters that we haven't really seen in the previous two Gospels. Luke makes comparisons throughout his Gospel of people who should be faithful and aren't with people who should not be faithful and are. As an example, value in society is placed on gender (men over women), age (old over young), and location (near Jerusalem over anywhere else). So Luke presents our first comparison with Zechariah (1. Male, 2. Old, 3. In the temple). We would expect Zechariah to be full of faith and honorable before God, but when Gabriel appears to him, he questions the message given and is mute for nine months. He is then compared to Mary (1. Female, 2. Young, 3. Nazareth [Inner City]). These two individuals could not be more different. If placed on a scale, Zechariah would be the clear fan favorite for faithful. Yet, when Gabriel comes to both of them, it is Mary who, in simple faith, receives the promise and offers herself as the Lord's servant.

Luke's Gospel calls us to re-examine our presuppositions and to see that God values everyone and does not make any distinction of age, class, or gender. You will see Luke do this throughout to demonstrate that the Kingdom of God does not have any of the same values as the kingdoms of the Earth. Luke's Gospel would have been received as scandalous to first century readers, but Luke is not concerned about this. He knows that Christ's Kingdom is the only Kingdom that matters. So in Luke, those classes who had been outcast by society are now depicted as the faithful of God.

We also see some aspects of the story of Jesus that we haven't seen in the previous Gospels. We see John's miraculous birth story with him leaping in his mother's womb when he encountered Jesus in his mother's womb. The shepherds are called out of the fields to bear witness to the birth of Christ while the Scribes and Pharisees lay sleeping in their beds. Jesus' dedication and the story of His first trip to Jerusalem for the Passover. Even babies and children are celebrated and seen as faithful here. For me, it's like looking into a kaleidoscope. There are new colors and patterns with every turn. Isn't it beautiful to know that in God's kingdom, people who would normally be discounted or forgotten are openly welcomed and celebrated? As He has said, "My ways are not your ways and my thoughts are not your thoughts..."

Finally, at the end of Luke 3, a Lukan genealogy of Jesus is reported. The genealogy starts with Jesus (family trees are traditionally "top-down"). We can see who Luke thinks is most important here. That genealogy does not adhere to the numerical or cultural rules used in Matthew's account. And realize that Jesus' line doesn't end with Abraham...it keeps going all the way back to the beginning...straight to God. So we know that Jesus is not the property of any group of people. Jesus is traced to God so we all feel connected to Him. He is the descendant of Adam, so are we! We are in Jesus' family, too.

No special people, no special gender, no special age, no special location. In Luke, Jesus has come to embody and to deliver Good News to everyone!

REFLECTIONS

1. What does it mean to you to see Luke including and celebrating marginalized groups as examples of faithfulness?

2. Luke used his platform to affect change in the way that marginalized people are portrayed and perceived. What can we do today to make life better for those who are marginalized today (immigrants, the poor, ethnic minorities, etc.)?

Day 17

THE UNPOPULAR COMMANDMENT | LUKE 4-6

"Love your enemies! Do good to them. Lend to them without expecting to be repaid. Then your reward from heaven will be very great, and you will truly be acting as children of the Most High, for he is kind to those who are unthankful and wicked. You must be compassionate, just as your father is compassionate."

- Luke 6:35

As a child, I had some challenging days around the dinner table. Although not every day was a bad one, my particularly rough days traditionally had something to do with a number of unsavory vegetables. Of particular difficulty were broccoli and okra. Something about their smell, taste, and consistency would make me nauseous every time. I can't tell you how many times I actually made honest attempts to eat them, but my throat was ready with a gag reflex. My mother wanted to communicate that she meant business. She told me sternly, "You will not leave the table until those vegetables are finished." I sat there for what seemed an eternity. I finally decided that because I wasn't leaving, I may as well take a nap. I pushed my plate aside, folded my arms, and went to sleep. On those days, I wished I was one of the "unfortunate children" people always spoke about who didn't have anything to eat. Certainly they were in a better position than I was during those times. I also prayed that God would stop the production of these awful vegetables. I was sure I prayed on behalf of the millions of children around the world taking naps next to their plates.

Reading the passage above takes me back to those days. I read through the words of Jesus and His expectation of me concerning my enemies and there is a visceral reaction in my heart. My mind plays through a thousand potential scenarios; me being taken advantage of, my being unappreciated. What if they actually do slap me? Who will take up for me? There is nothing pleasant or attractive about this. I want to raise my hand sheepishly and ask Jesus, "May I be excused?" Why in the world would Jesus place that sort of "vegetable" on my plate? As I read through the words of Jesus, I am convinced that His commands are actually indicative of His own character. When I read, Jesus hasn't assembled a list of random recommendations. Jesus is actually describing the way He deals with His own enemies and the enemies of His father. On a daily basis, Heaven dispenses life force to those who will utilize said force to persecute the Kingdom. Rain and sunshine are equally distributed to villains and criminals right along with the Saints. So, everyone receives something they do not deserve, at some point in time. There have been days that I was an enemy of Heaven, and God still gave good things to me. To be honest, it was that kind of undeserved love that has drawn, and continues to draw, me into relationship with Jesus. As I consider what Jesus as done, I really want to be more honorable to Him.

Then, I'm stopped in my tracks...

The undeserved treatment I extend to my enemies is God's appeal. In the same way that I am drawn to Christ when I realized how good He is to me when I don't deserve it, God wants my good treatment of people who treat me poorly to be His appeal to them? Wow. I must honestly say, I don't fully know how it works. I don't know how not to open myself to abuse by being kind to my abuser. I don't know how to prevent being taken advantage of by crooks and thieves...but God does. And perhaps, if I'm leaning on Him and praying to Him at all times and asking for strength and guidance, and for a quadruple portion of His Spirit each day to go into these situations, and to replicate His character so I say and do what He would versus my preferences, He will show me how it's done.

In fact, what if that's the point? Perhaps I'm placed in these situations to keep me on my knees, dependent on Him, trusting in Him. And my enemies end up being God's appeal to me as well. Just wow.

REFLECTIONS

1. Have you ever found yourself blessed after blessing an enemy?

2. What does Jesus' interaction with enemies model for us when dealing with our own?

HE WON'T LET GO!
| LUKE 7-9

"Soon afterward Jesus began a tour of the nearby towns and villages, preaching and announcing the Good News about the Kingdom of God. He took His twelve disciples with him, along with some women who had been cured of evil spirits and diseases. Among them was Mary Magdalene, from whom he had cast out seven demons;"

- Luke 8:1, 2

"I will know everything I need to know about you if you show me your friends." We've heard such adages over and over. Essentially, the reputation and character of the company we keep dictates our own personality and character. Jesus was repeatedly criticized for the company He kept. He hung out with criminals and drunkards so much, He was called a drunk Himself. I can imagine an older man or woman pulling Jesus to the side and saying, "You've gotta watch who you hang around, baby." Still, Jesus gravitates to those living at the fringes of society. The focus of many sermons and stories highlight Jesus' pattern of choosing sketchy friends, demonstrated by the twelve. But my gaze wanders to the nature of the women He keeps company with, namely Mary Magdalene. Now, if Jesus was criticized for the men he kept company with, I can only imagine what was said about His proximity to Mary.

She had been known for her immorality. Mary's issues were so bad, she was said to have been possessed by seven demons. Men and women walked wide circles around her, afraid others would see them near her and ask questions. At several places in scripture, we seen the way people made an example of her and shamed her publicly. Yet, Jesus seems unbothered by her presence. I'd like to suggest that Jesus keeps Mary around precisely because He wants us to draw conclusions. Jesus actually wants us to make judgements about Him by the presence of this woman. He is communicating something to us intentionally. First, Jesus demonstrates He is a friend of sinners. Jesus is committed to Mary, even in times when she is not committed to Him. Secondly, we can look at the number seven; that number can either be an actual number or a symbolic number. Seven means perfection or a completed cycle. Either Jesus went in on seven different occasions and cast out demons, or Jesus cast out seven demons at one time, or the version I prefer, Jesus kept casting out demons from Mary for as long as it took.

When I think about myself, I have had some challenges that were far less heavy than Mary's. I have asked for forgiveness on several occasions, and have found that forgiveness and restoration each time I've asked for it. I believe that Jesus kept working with Mary for as long as it took for her to be fully healed and restored. Now, everywhere Jesus traveled and preached, standing just feet from Him is a living and breathing example of the true love and power that Jesus has toward us.

Now, every time Jesus preached, Mary could say within herself:

1. Jesus is not ashamed of me.

2. Jesus has power to heal and deliver me from even the worst habits and issues.

3. Jesus will keep working to fully restore me for as long as it takes.

I am so incredibly glad that Jesus is so generous with the friends He makes, and is willing to have me as one of them.

REFLECTIONS

1. What does Jesus' friendship with you say about His character?

2. How do we responsibly maintain relationships with people who could be blessed by our positive example?

HAVE A SEAT!
| LUKE 10-12

"But Martha was distracted by the big dinner she was preparing. She came to Jesus and said, 'Lord, doesn't it seem unfair to you that my sister just sits here while I do all the work? Tell her to come and help me.' But the Lord said to her, 'My dear Martha, you are worried and upset over all these details! There is only one thing worth being concerned about. Mary has discovered it, and it will not be taken away from her.'"

- Luke 10:40-42

They say, "Familiarity breeds contempt."

Jesus has been preaching and teaching around the region and decides to relax for a while at the home of Mary, Martha, and Lazarus in Bethany. The house is full, bubbling with laughter and conversation. Jesus always traveled with a crowd and anyone who hosted Him knew that having Him over would mean a great deal of work. As her guests enjoyed themselves, Martha went about seeing that everything was just right, buzzing through the house, stirring pots and setting tables as she always did. She enjoyed hosting and gladly did what was required to present the best experience possible.

She's counting spoons and forks, stirring punch, checking on biscuits in the oven, when she recognizes something… She's doing all of this work alone. I would imagine that Martha spun around the kitchen looking for her designated helper. She peeks out of the kitchen and sees her sister, smiling while sitting on the floor listening to the conversation. What was once a joy now felt like an inconvenience. Martha has been working her fingers to the bone to pull this dinner off, and her sister is sitting with the guests. "How dare she?" Martha thought. "With all of the work to be done she sits in the living room as though it will all get done by itself." Martha is so incensed, she puts all social etiquette to the side. She takes off her apron, drops the spoon, and marches into the living room to set things straight.

"JESUS!"

Silence falls upon the room and everyone turns to hear where this address came from. "Don't you care that I am left to do all this work by myself, while my sister just sits at your feet?"

I believe that a fundamental flaw of humanity is the tendency to presume what God cares about. Some days ago, we reviewed this scenario when the disciples asked Jesus, "Don't you care that we are going to drown?" The question presumes that the questioner has an answer the person being questioned has not considered. Those disciples wanted Jesus to put His hands on a bucket to help secure a sail. They wanted to know why Jesus would not participate in the process of surviving the storm, as Jesus, calm and peaceful, sleeps through it. Maybe Jesus doesn't care. Maybe Jesus doesn't "care" because the thought or possibility that has the disciples, and Martha, panicking is only a figment of their imagination. Jesus had just fed 5000 men, not including women and children, with five loaves of bread with two fish. He'd also taken jars filled with water and, with a prayer, made wine superior to the product of any winery. While Martha is stressing herself to prepare a meal for twenty people, the guest of honor has taken a small boy's lunch and fed a stadium.

Maybe Jesus doesn't care.

Martha comes to Jesus angry, offended, and stressed because Jesus will not indulge her attempt to fix something with painstaking effort that He can resolve with a word. How many times have we been in Martha's shoes?: Dirty apron with hair sweated-out, hand on hip, standing in the middle of the room where Jesus is sitting. Because we feel we have the moral upper hand, we do not bother with the pleasantries or reverence. We want an answer to why Jesus has not helped us to fix this by ourselves.

I'm so glad Jesus is merciful...

"Martha, Martha... You are concerned over so many things. But Mary has chosen the best part, and it will not be taken away from her."

What if the things you're doing to try and serve the Lord are actually standing in the way of true fellowship with Him? What if the things you've placed so much importance on, the things that have to get done, are actually a distraction from where you need to be?

Certainly, Jesus cares...but it's a little different than you think.

REFLECTIONS

1. What frustrations have caused you to question God?

2. Are there areas where you can do more sitting at Jesus' feet than "preparing meals?"

JUST FOR ONE...
| LUKE 13-15

*"Tax collectors and other notorious sinners often came t
listen to Jesus teach. 2. This made the Pharisees and teachers
of religious law complain that he was associating with such
sinful people—even eating with them! 3. So Jesus told them
this story: 4. 'If a man has a hundred sheep and one of them
gets lost, what will he do? Won't he leave the ninety-nine others in the wilderness and go to search for the one that is lost
until he finds it? 5. And when he has found it, he will joyfully
carry it home on his shoulders. 6. When he arrives, he will call
together his friends and neighbors, saying, 'Rejoice with me
because I have found my lost sheep.' 7. In the same way, there
is more joy in heaven over one lost sinner who repents and
returns to God than over ninety-nine others who are
righteous and haven't strayed away!'"*

- Luke 15:1-7

I have an annoying tendency to lose things.

About four months ago, I purchased a brand new iPad mini.
I didn't really need it, I think I was simply filling an internal
electronic quota. I bought the newest model with sufficient proces-
sor speed and memory, and marveled at the clarity of its screen. My
old one had been beat up pretty badly, so I was happy to welcome a

newer, and prettier, model. I do a host of things on my iPad, not the least of which is reading books. It's pretty handy to have a library of books and music on hand so I can read them while I wait.

I remember running errands and reading as I went about my day. I got a great deal of work done and went about my business. I found myself looking through my purse, one afternoon, trying to place my hand on my iPad and it wasn't there. I didn't think anything about it. I figured I probably left it in the car, between my seat and center console, as I often have. I casually looked for it; I was certain it was safe. I left town for a couple of days, thought about it but went along with business as usual. I returned home and decided to really look for that iPad and it wasn't anywhere. I looked in my car, in my office, I checked for it in my purses and bags, I called every place I could think of. No iPad. Not only did I have no clue where the tablet was, I had no clue of when I'd lost it. I had no clue where to even look. Then I panicked.

Have you ever lost something precious?

Jesus has been accused of fraternizing with the wrong people. He's been spending time with tax collectors and prostitutes and the so-called righteous Scribes and Pharisees are incensed. "How could someone who claims to be righteous spend time with such scum?" They reasoned. "If Jesus was who he says he is, he'd never waste his time on losers like them." Jesus' response demonstrates for us that His heart for the lost is much larger than we'd anticipated.

A man has 100 sheep and realizes that one of them is unaccounted for. That's only a 1% loss. I suspect, if those sheep are only regarded as a source of income, the shepherd would only have put in minimal effort to recover it. There were still ninety-nine safe and happy ones that were where they were supposed to be. Yet, the shepherd sets out, leaving the ninety-nine, to find the one. Shepherds spend so much time with each of their sheep, they become more like friends and family than income. The shepherd sleeps in the same space as the sheep. He personally leads them to food and water. When the sheep get sick or infected with lice or fleas, it's the shepherd who personally cleans them and restores them to health. The shepherd also knows each sheep individually. He has a different relationship with each one, dependent on their needs. The sheep and shepherd are so intimately acquainted that two herds can be mixed together, grazing in a field and a shepherd will call for his flock. The sheep that belong to him will come at the sound of his voice alone. So when this shepherd sets out to find the lost sheep, he's not looking for revenue, he's looking for his child.

Think for a moment how you tear your house up for a lost set of keys, or for a check you haven't had time to cash. Now, think of how you look for your child, or the child of a loved one when they are lost. Both efforts are intense and thorough, but one lost item can be replaced, the other is irreplaceable. Not just tangibly irreplaceable, but parents search knowing that mentally and emotionally, a child can never be replaced. That is how the shepherd looks for his sheep. That is how Jesus looks for me!

It's no wonder why Jesus keeps company with such "scum"...because the people we regard as "scum" are His babies. He knows their names and stories and thoughts, and the flock is just not right until they have been restored to the fold. Jesus is not satisfied until they come home.

It was eight weeks later when I prayed that God would show me where my iPad was. That evening, I had an overwhelming desire to go to the mall and find a dress. I went and looked, but I found nothing. I was leaving the mall and felt impressed to have my eyebrows threaded...Um...okay. I could use that. As I sat in the chair being serviced, I felt an overwhelming impression to ask the woman arching my eyebrows if she'd found an iPad. I thought it was ridiculous, so I didn't say anything. She finished the service and as I approached the counter to pay, I heard the Spirit shout, "Ask her about a missing iPad!" I sheepishly paid and mustered a whisper, "Um, have you found a lost iPad?" The woman looked at me and began to speak to someone in the back in a different language. She then asked about how long ago the iPad was lost, what size it was, and what color it was. I described the iPad to the best of my recollection and held my breath. She opened her front drawer and reached deep into the space to unearth a very dusty, but familiar...iPad. When I tell you I shouted in that place! I shouted and danced a little, over an iPad I'd lost.

If I was nearly sick and anxious over something I spent a few hundred dollars on, how much more is Christ absolutely bent to do everything in His power to ensure His babies are found?

REFLECTIONS

1. What can we do to help Jesus' lost sheep to make it back home?

2. Describe how you feel when you consider how passionate God is about you being found.

WHAT ARE YOU WORKIN' WITH? | LUKE 16-18

"Here's the lesson: Use your worldly resources to benefit others and make friends. Then, when your earthly possessions are gone, they will welcome you to an eternal home. If you are faithful in the little things, you will be faithful in large ones. But if you are dishonest in little things, you won't be honest with greater responsibilities."

- Luke 16: 9, 10

When assessing our faithfulness, everything counts...
The more I interact with Scripture, the more I am continually intrigued by the mind of Jesus. I've been reading as He instructs His followers on the nature of true love and devotion to the Kingdom of God. He's freeing people from oppression, physical and spiritual, and alerts us that that kind of power is a natural byproduct of connection with the God of Heaven. But this is a curveball for me. Jesus tells of a shrewd servant who scurries to network when he learns he will be fired. This man adjusts the accounts for all his master's debtors so that each of them will have lower amounts to pay. He has the ability to make the changes so he uses

his access to create an inroads for future opportunities. It is a brilliant idea, though his master will end up receiving less than he had loaned to his debtors. This man uses what he has to get what he wants. And Jesus says, this guy is savvier than most in the Kingdom.

It's one of those conversations you have with an older aunt or uncle that make you squirm in your seat. I can imagine blushing a bit when Jesus told this story. "Is he really saying this?" I find myself reviewing His words to see if I've missed anything. Jesus is saying this guy is brilliant because he found a way to make a sour situation work for him. He cut some corners and 'cooked the books' but he worked it out. "You should be more like that!" Although I totally get what Jesus is saying, I'm truly not expecting these concepts to come from Him. Jesus wants His followers to be better business people. He wants us to be smarter about how we allocate our resources and how we network. Jesus wants us to be intentional about the way we handle our business dealings. My family members used to say, "Don't be so heavenly minded that you're no earthly good."

I've often adopted the mindset that because Jesus would be coming soon, I didn't need to be mindful about how I handled my resources. "Jesus paid it all" was my mantra. But Jesus is cautioning me that this approach will not get me any closer to the kingdom. A lack of wisdom with my resources will not only eliminate opportunities in the earth but will also be counted against me in Heaven. God expects me to be "faithful" not just in spiritual things but also with the things I've been given. Jesus is counting my deeds and my dimes. Jesus presents the parable to share a principle: If you are faithful in little things, you will be faithful in larger ones. But dishonesty in little things shows you will be dishonest in larger responsibilities. I always saw this in connection with spiritual responsibility, but following this conversation, Jesus seems to be referring to opportunity and responsibility that aren't necessarily religious. It seems that Jesus promises greater financial, civic, and public opportunities to those who are diligent with the smaller opportunities.

Jesus expects me to make the most of every opportunity? Wow!

And Jesus seems to suggest that He will work along with the "powers that be" to provide larger opportunities to those who have proven to be responsible with the smaller chances they'd been given. What a new and fresh perspective from the words of Jesus. Jesus calls us to be righteous and diligent. Then, when I've been diligent with the small thing, I'll be given something larger. The question we now have to pose is: What opportunities have I been given? Where has God given me exposure and resources? How am I relating to those opportunities? Have I been giving my best? Next: What relationships have I been blessed with? How am I leveraging those relationships? Am I maximizing their benefit and doing all I can to make them work for me? I then have to repent for the responsibilities I've shirked and opportunities I've squandered in the name of being spiritual. Jesus is concerned about each and every aspect of my life. I must covenant to be both a righteous woman and a savvy business woman. This is how I honor God with all my soul, might, strength, heart, and mind.

REFLECTIONS

1. How do you begin to balance being spiritual and successful?

2. What opportunities do you have access to that need more of your effort, time, and attention?

HE KNOWS MY NAME
| LUKE 19-21

"And Jesus said unto him, 'This day is salvation come to this house, forsomuch as he also is a Son of Abraham. For the Son of man is come to seek and to save that which was lost.'"

- Luke 19: 9, 10

Another ordinary day...

Zacchaeus had been about his business, filing and collecting taxes. He had done this for years and his countrymen hated to see him coming. I don't know that the IRS (U.S. Bureau of Taxation) enjoys a better reception today. When Zacchaeus came, the people knew they would be robbed in the name of the law. Zacchaeus enjoyed a great income and had all the money he could have ever wanted or needed. He felt empty inside with a void that all the fine delicacies in the world couldn't fill. He's decked in fine clothing with rings on each finger. If someone weren't looking closely, they would mistake him for royalty, but upon further examination, they'd see that was just Zacchaeus, crook in a suit. For all his fashion and opulence, Zacchaeus felt something was missing. The Bible tells us that Zacchaeus was conducting his business for the day and heard that Jesus was passing by. Something about Jesus drew Zacchaeus' attention. He wasn't blind or lame, he didn't have a disease that needed to be healed, or anything... but there was something he couldn't put his finger on, something he thought Jesus may also be able to fill.

A short man, it didn't take long for Zacchaeus to realize that he would be swallowed up in the crowd that approached him. So many people clamoring to touch Jesus and to hear what he had to say. Zacchaeus was ordinarily a very proud man who never had to get dirty, but today, Zacchaeus didn't care about his clothes. He had felt an emotion that he'd never felt. Desperation. He sees the crowd growing ever closer and he has to think fast...the tree! He could see Jesus if he would climb the tree! Something inside him whispered, "Are you really going to climb that filthy tree? What if people see you? What if you tear your new robes?" But something about Jesus was more important than his robes or his pride.

"Maybe you should schedule a meeting! Certainly you can still hear His way of thinking and compliment His success in a private conversation." But Zacchaeus knew he wasn't worthy to receive such a man as this. But he would get as close to Him as he could. He would not miss this. Zacchaeus, probably a plump man (a sign of wealth) and not regularly acquainted with exercise, scurried up the tree with great effort. There are twigs in his hair. He's torn his robe. Probably scraped an arm or leg trying to get up the tree, but he is there, secured in a spot where he could see and hear what Jesus had to say as He passed by. I imagine his head and hands began to sweat. He probably wondered if he looked ridiculous or if people who knew him would see him up there, in a tree. But the thought of seeing the Jesus he'd heard about was enough to keep him in his spot. The crowd walked with Jesus and although you could hear their many footsteps, the voice you could hear very clearly was the voice of Jesus. He was teaching and though the crowd had been moving forward at a steady pace, they seemed to slow down as they moved closer to that tree. Zacchaeus probably felt his heart begin to pound as Jesus stopped with that crowd, and looks up.

What an exciting, yet terrifying, moment when Jesus looks at us. It's one thing for Him to be in the neighborhood or doing work in and around someone else, but what excitement mixed with wonder I feel when I become aware that Jesus has a conversation, a word for me.

Jesus and Zacchaeus' eyes meet and then Jesus calls Zacchaeus by name...

"Zacchaeus, come down, I'm eating at your house today."

Joy rushed through his soul as before he knew it, Zacchaeus had made it down the tree in a fraction of the time it had taken for him to climb it. Zacchaeus smiled, even giggled a bit, as he escorted Jesus to his home. Was this real? After all Zacchaeus had done, he knew he didn't deserve this honor.

There are times when God is so interested in seeing us saved that salvation comes to our house. As the 23rd Psalm expresses, "Surely goodness and mercy shall follow me all the days of my life." Those moments where we know we have used our 100th shot and have failed, yet we feel God smiling over us anyway. Those times where we don't even feel worthy to be in the same space as the Master, yet we notice Jesus looking at us anyway. But it's not a look of condemnation but a look of compassion. Zacchaeus was so overwhelmed that he made an announcement. It wasn't something he'd planned to do. He is so grateful for Jesus' kindness, he is moved to show his appreciation. He essentially gives away every bit of money he has. For the first time in his life, he doesn't think money is important. He is not concerned about any of the fine things his shenanigans have allowed him to purchase. He has now found something more important than his money and possessions and he is not going to ever let it go.

REFLECTIONS

What has Jesus' visitation done for you? Have you found yourself in the presence of the Christ and felt impressed to do something about it? What do you feel compelled to give in response to what God has given you? Perhaps you feel compelled to give the ultimate gift, your life! No matter the sacrifice, we can rejoice, because salvation has come to our house today!

Day 23

EVEN ME | LUKE 22-24

"One of the criminals hanging beside him scoffed, 'So you're the Messiah, are you? Prove it by saving yourself– and us, too, while you're at it!'

But the other criminal protested, 'Don't you fear God even when you have been sentenced to die? We deserve to die for our crimes, but this man hasn't done anything wrong.' Then he said to Jesus, 'Remember me when you come into your Kingdom.'

And Jesus replied, 'I assure you, today, you will be with me in Paradise.'"

- Luke 23: 39-43

I've heard many stories of the experiences people have the last moments before death. Many of these stories have been told by some who have been very close to death and recovered. Some have said they saw a white light, much like the light that shines from the end of a long tunnel. Others have reported seeing figures like angels, hovering around their beds and outside of their window. Although I would imagine those moments would be torturous and laden with fear, many have reported an incredible sense of peace that overwhelmed them. Even though the process is a lot different than I'd expect it to be, for most of us, death is not a welcomed friend but a dreaded enemy. I can only imagine the anxiety they all felt. Three men, three different stories, one shared fate. The crowd gathered, heckling them all. The crucifixion, while grim, served as entertainment for those who could stomach it. The soldiers threw dice to see who would get the possessions of the men being executed. They didn't particularly care that they'd be enjoying the wares of dead men. In their estimation, this was just another crucifixion, they may as well get something for their time. While the hustle and bustle of the event carried on below, a conversation ensued above. Seemingly deflecting from his own situation, one of the thieves being executed began to taunt Jesus. He had probably heard about Jesus' work around Jerusalem and found it amusing that He could perform miracles on behalf of others yet He didn't work out an escape from this fate, for Himself. Surely, he thought Jesus was just a phony and was no better than himself. So because he had nothing better to do, he joined in the hecklings being slung at Jesus.

The other thief saw something different. He saw an innocent man being treated in a way that wasn't earned. This thief felt he deserved his penalty. He had done the crime and he was fully aware that he was now reaping the consequences. But when he looked at Jesus, he perceived something was very different about this man.

"We deserve to be here," the enlightened thief shot back. "We've earned this, but this man is innocent! Don't you fear God, even now?" This thief's eyes had been opened just long enough for him to see his true condition along with the identity of the man hanging next to him. This thief hadn't been a good man. He didn't have a stellar record to refer to. But stealing had taught him how to discern an opportunity. He was a pro at noticing an opening. As he defended the honor of this man, a notion occurred to him. If what people said He called himself was true, and if He was really the powerful Man others had spoken about, maybe He did have an inside track on the afterlife. This thief could use another chance to make something of himself. So, he makes a request with no theological foundation or spiritual coaching.

"Jesus, remember me when you come into your Kingdom."

Just like that, in the final hours of his life, this man decided that he wanted to be a part of Jesus' entourage. We expect that there would be some hoops the man had to jump through or demonstration that was necessary to prove he was sincere in his request. Surely he needed a trial period of faithfulness, with his track record. But Jesus requires no such thing. He is not concerned with a fully ripened plant in this moment, just a seed that has found a resting place in good ground. That's all that was required.

Jesus replied, "I assure you, today, you will be with me in paradise."

How could Jesus feel so comfortable, extending that type of guarantee to a man whose record has been so deplorable? Simple, Jesus can accept this man because his own sacrifice is sufficient to cover all that this man has done and would ever do in the future. His sacrifice is all sufficient! Though he lived a thief, he could now die with the assurance that Jesus would take care of his eternal debt. This is the assurance we all can have in Jesus, that our belief in Him is all we need to actually experience eternal life. A simple request fueled by faith actually gives thieves like you and me the keys to God's Kingdom. The question is, do you believe and receive it?

REFLECTIONS

1. Do you have an assurance of salvation right now? Do you believe that Christ's death is sufficient to pay the debt for all your sin?

2. If you haven't asked Jesus to forgive and cleanse your sin, are you ready to ask today?

Day 24

SHINE A LIGHT ON ME
| JOHN 1-3

"The Word gave life to everything that was created, and his life brought light to everyone. The light shines in the darkness, and the darkness can never extinguish it."

- John 1: 4, 5

Well, not everyone is looking for a Savior, Lord, King, or Messiah; everyone knows what it's like to look for "light."

John is the last of the disciples. He's been confined to the island cabinets, a penal colony. He has not committed any major crime. He is not considered armed and dangerous. John is on Patmos because the powers that be have tried their most sadistic schemes to kill him and they won't work. Can I rejoice in knowing that when God wants me alive, no demon in hell can do otherwise? John is on Patmos Island, and while he can't preach or testify, he can write. He takes the task of sharing the gospel with the non-religious people of the day. Those individuals are Gnostic... more philosophical than religious. They entertain concepts pertaining to the duality of life and believe that all physical and metaphysical realities have a direct opposite. The concepts they entertained: light vs. darkness, flesh vs. spirit, and good vs. evil. Everything they assessed was judged according to these theories. The favorable side of those comparisons was attributed to the gods, the negatives to the evil ones. So, John is tasked with sharing the good news of Jesus with these thinkers. John needs to tell this story from a perspective they would understand. So he uses a metaphor we can relate to even today… light. Not only did Jesus come to shed light, but Jesus Himself also is the light.

For our reflection today, consider what it means that Jesus is the light over your life. What situations are you facing that could use a little light? What places are you stumbling over because you can't properly see your way? The story of Jesus will be presented to us in a way very different from the other accounts. Let us receive John's final snapshot of the Lord Jesus and allow Him to shine His light into our hearts.

REFLECTIONS

1. What can we learn from John about sharing the good news of Jesus with those who don't have a religious background?

2. What areas of your life could use the light of Heaven?

NOT WHAT WE EXPECTED,
| JOHN 4-6

*"Jesus replied, 'I tell you the truth, you want to be
with me because I fed you, not because you understood the
miraculous signs. But don't be so concerned about perishable
things like food. Spend your energy seeking the eternal life
that the Son of Man can give you. For God the Father has given
me the seal of his approval.' They replied, 'We want to perform
God's works, too. What should we do?' Jesus told them,
'This is the only work God wants from you:
Believe in the one He has sent.'"*

- John 6:26-29

J esus has been ministering through his preaching as well as performing miracles. At this point, his reputation amassed a huge crowd who followed Jesus virtually everywhere. The traditional preacher would find comfort in that, knowing that people wanted to see and hear them. Crowds can be intoxicating and can give the sense that the preacher is really effective. There is something reassuring about having a large group of followers. The gathering of the group can, if we're not careful, become the ruler by which success is measured. It's no wonder Jesus purges his crowd. With the recent media treatment of any sort of "purge," I know that may seem like a harsh term, but when you hear Jesus' dialogue in John 6, it seems that He actually wanted to whittle His crowd down. Some would call His sermon "career suicide." Jesus lines the crowd up and preaches a Word that is guaranteed to push people away. It is confusing. Why would Jesus want to push people away?

First, Jesus is not concerned about masses. He does not derive His sense of worth nor effectiveness from the amount of people who show-up to see Him. Because Jesus is secure, He can concern Himself with motive. Jesus knows the majority of those following him are only looking for another meal. The question is "Will they follow Jesus after the meals stop flowing?" Up until a few minutes ago, even I wasn't totally clear as to why Jesus would handle these people this way. Isn't it normal to be hungry? Why is Jesus so harsh with people who actually need to eat and who are connecting with Jesus to ensure they stay fed? The more I read, I realize that Jesus understands the nature of following Him and that there will certainly be days when there will be no meals. There would be days when faithfulness will demand that these people not only endure hunger, but that they also be perfectly okay with those meals not flowing. So Jesus, in mercy, tells them that the Kingdom He is building is not for them.

Not today.

But doesn't Jesus want people to follow Him?

Well, it depends...

I live in an area where construction is ongoing. There are several high-rise buildings being built and my guess is that those companies that contracted these projects intend to have people live and work in those buildings. Although it will be safe to live and walk in those towers in time, until the work is completed on those structures, it would be incredibly dangerous for me to walk through them, unprotected, in their unfinished state. The hazards of that trip would require that I wear protective gear. If I were to fall or, worse yet, if something were to fall on me at a time when I wasn't wearing protective gear, I could be seriously hurt or killed. Even though life as a disciple during these days would have had some immense benefits, there would be some temptations and attacks those followers would necessarily have to face. Satan is trying everything possible to stop Jesus from completing His mission on Earth. This means that those closest to Him would receive the brunt of those attacks as well. What if "faith" or "belief" was the protective gear that insulates the disciples of Jesus from the full brunt of the attacks Satan will launch? Consider it this way; it would actually be dangerous for unprotected people to stay on. They could be seriously hurt or killed. So, Jesus preaches a message that only those who believe, or wearing hard hats, will be able to survive. Better for them to be nudged away by Jesus than to be wiped away by the enemy. Just wow...

Let's think about something before we close. Some elements in this scenario have not changed. Although we may not be looking for fish and loaves, there are times when we equate Jesus' faithfulness to us with the maintenance of the health and well-being of ourselves and those we love. If we're not careful, we can be following Jesus because of what He can do for us, rather than our simple belief in Him. Now is a good time to check our motivation. Are we angry or annoyed with Jesus because our prayer has not been answered in as quick a fashion as we wanted? Do we hold God hostage to our demands then leave when we aren't satisfied with His answer? If we demand that God answer our way...right away...it is very possible that we are no better than the hundreds of people who left Jesus that day. May God help us to follow because of who He is, and not for what He can provide.

REFLECTIONS

1. "What would your connection with God be like if you never received another major blessing?

2. Could you still serve the Lord if he didn't answer another of your prayers in the way you'd prefer?

CHOOSING FREEDOM | JOHN 7-9

*"Jesus said to the people who believed in him,
'You are truly my disciples if you remain faithful to my teachings. And you will know the truth, and the truth will set you free.'" 'But we are descendants of Abraham,' they said. 'We have never been slaves to anyone. What do you mean, 'You will be set free?' Jesus replied, 'I tell you the truth, everyone who sins is a slave of sin. A slave is not a permanent member of the family, but a son is part of the family forever.
So if the Son sets you free, you are truly free.'"*

- John 8:31-36

"I freed a thousand slaves. I could have freed a thousand more if only they knew they were slaves."

- Harriet Tubman

Have you ever known someone in a bad situation? Of all the counsel and effort I've given, the most frustrating and painstaking of my experiences have been with people who were unaware that their situation was dangerous. It's uncanny; at some point in our conversations, the person will begin to either deny their issue or defend it. Rather than proposing solutions to their challenge, most of the conversation is spent convincing the poor victim that their state isn't ideal. We learned, in John 1, that when Jesus, "the light," came into the world, the darkness of the world was so dense the light could do little to dispel it. This conversation is a case-in-point. Jesus is speaking to a group of Jews who actually believed in Him. They have heard His sermons and benefitted from His miracles and received the truths He has presented, to this point. Though they have enjoyed His company, Jesus knows that they have not received the true benefit of His presence. Although they are satisfied with their current relationship, Jesus knows they need something deeper. Rather than being their benefactor, Jesus wants to become their Lord. He lets them know that while they feel free, they are, in fact, slaves. Given the history of Israel and the powerful story of their deliverance from Egypt, Jews take a great deal of pride in their independence. Couple this with the fact that slaves in their culture were seen as the bottom of society. Slaves were conquered people either by war or by circumstance. To be a slave meant a person or group was unable to manage their own situations and became the prey of someone richer and stronger. Stripped of all personal dignity and rights, slaves were seen as the least desirable of all people. To have been called a slave was the harshest insult a person could receive. All of that being considered, Jesus called them "slaves." The believers are incensed. They liked Jesus well enough, but He had offended them in the highest possible sense. Their pride is bruised, their anger is piqued, and their true hearts have been exposed. They were willing to believe in Jesus as long as His words didn't offend them or challenge their deeply held beliefs. This brings us to a very key principle. There is a real, yet often, imperceptible danger that our closely held beliefs will create a barrier between the Lord and us. We feel that we are devout because we live according to our regulations. However, when the deep and dark areas of our character are challenged, we scurry away and protect what has been threatened. This is the definition of slavery. As long as there are unyielding places in our hearts and minds, no matter how much we believe, we will always retreat when they are challenged, even when challenged by Jesus Himself.

Because of love, Jesus exposes those chains; beliefs that keep us from fully surrendering to Him and grants us freedom. Our choice is whether we will be ruled by our preferences or surrender to Christ. Do we prefer our mindsets or our Savior? Jesus lets us know that He has the power to make us free. Because He is the heir to all power and authority, Christ can break any and all chains that limit us, even the chains in our own minds. Surrendering to Jesus means we can be free, today.

COMMITMENT

Even today, Jesus is setting people free from ideas and prejudices that keep us from living to the fullest. If we ask, Jesus can expose every area that keeps us enslaved. We can be free, right now, if we just ask. Take some time in prayer to share with God the areas of your life where you need to experience freedom. Surrender those things to him and begin trusting that He can still free you from even the deepest challenge.

JUMPING TO CONCLUSIONS | JOHN 10-12

"Then she returned to Mary. She called Mary aside from the mourners and told her, 'The Teacher is here and wants to see you.' So Mary immediately went to him.

Jesus had stayed outside the village, at the place where Martha met him. When the people who were at the house consoling Mary saw her leave so hastily, they assumed she was going to Lazarus' grave to weep. So they followed her there. When Mary arrived and saw Jesus, she fell at his feet and said, 'Lord, if only you had been here, my brother would not have died.'

When Jesus saw her weeping and saw the other people wailing with her, a deep anger welled up within him, and he was deeply troubled."

- John 10:28-33

What I hear, see, and feel have an uncanny knack of making me feel I know what's going on. Have you found yourself watching a television show closely? I have several shows that I follow and tend to know the major themes of the programs. The shows I watch are well-written so on more than one occasion, I have believed I knew exactly what was happening and what parties were involved, only to learn that my, seemingly, well-founded conclusions were more than hasty judgements. It seems that the writers of programs know that to maintain interest and to build viewership, an occasional plot twist is necessary every now and then. It seems that it's the same with Jesus. John is showing us yet another snapshot of the Savior that the other Gospels hadn't covered. It's an insider account of the raising of Lazarus; a miracle that solidly planted Jesus' power deeply in the minds of all who had attended Lazarus' funeral and then saw him walking through town four days later. What an incredible testimony!

Of all the people Jesus could have performed that miracle for, His most masterful display...it would naturally be the privilege of His friends...right? But to make it to the miracle...Lazarus had to die. Grief and loss leave most of us asking a lot of questions. Many of the questions revolve around the belief that faith in God should eliminate us from the experience of loss or evil. There is actually no scriptural example to demonstrate that principle, however. In fact, the most devout figures in scripture all underwent some sort of major trauma that tested their loyalty to God and that ultimately proved God's amazing faithfulness.

So, if they had to go through it, what makes us think we should be excused?

Mary is utterly angry with Jesus because she feels His absence was cold and heartless. She lodges one of the most chilling accusations I've heard in scripture: "Lord, if only you had been here, my brother would not have died." Wow...

First, she doesn't know that. Perhaps her brother died because he lacked faith to get well. Hmm... Certainly a possibility. What if Jesus' delay was an act of faith to bypass a lack of faith Lazarus would have been able to think or voice, had he been alive? Hmm... Secondly, Mary assumes that death is a factor when Jesus is involved. Like, when Jesus is present, who cares that someone died? It hurts, inconvenient...but certainly not a problem Jesus can't address. Here's my epiphany, when I panic and find myself shaking my fist at Heaven, it's because I feel that my circumstance is now out of range of God's power. I wanted to prevent things from going beyond a certain point and once they have ascended to that height. I give up hope that God can do anything about it. It's where my most egregious sins have been generated, right in the place of hurt and disappointment that came from God letting something go to a place I wanted to avoid.

REFLECTIONS

I wonder if Jesus gets frustrated with me, too. Does Jesus' blood pressure rise as my faith disintegrates? Is He shaking His head at me while I shake my fist at Him? Certainly, because the truth is, I know enough about Jesus to know that there is no obstacle I can approach that He can't decimate. Rather than asking how or when this obstacle will be dealt with, I will concentrate on who is with me.

Day 28

I'LL BE BACK
| JOHN 13-15

"Don't let your hearts be troubled. Trust in God, and trust also in me. There is more than enough room in my Father's home. If this were not so, would I have told you that I am going to prepare a place for you? When everything is ready, I will come and get you, so that you will always be with me where I am."

- John 14: 1-3

Another memory from my childhood is staying home as my mom went out for errands or to an event, solo. I'm certain with three small children, she occasionally needed some fresh air. So she would leave my sisters and me home with our father while she got out for a little while. While she prepared to leave, my imagination went wild with all the fun she would have, without us. I was certain there would be funnel cakes and Ferris wheels all along the route to her destination. I'm unsure where I gathered this information because during the times I had been permitted to go along, we were usually bored and tired of walking after a short while. Still, whenever I was being left behind, I was sure it was because she was going to do something exciting without me.

It isn't fun to be left out.

As an adult, I've become more comfortable with spending time alone. If I want amusement or to have a good time, I can arrange that by myself. Still, there are moments where I imagine the fun and excitement people are having without me. Human nature desires inclusion. Most people desire a place where they are a part of an inner circle and where they feel irreplaceable. The television series "Cheers" articulated this desire with its theme song:

Where everybody knows your name.
And they're always glad you came.
You want to be where people see,
People are all the same.
You want to go where everybody knows your name.

The group of people chronicled in the series had their need filled by going to the same bar every evening after work. We may not spend our evenings drinking and sharing the details of our days, but we tend to crave that sort of "sacred space." I believe the disciples enjoyed that sense of longing during their time walking closely with the Savior. It had been 3-1/2 years and to this point, they had been invited to accompany Jesus most times. They enjoyed being part of His inner circle and experiencing His miracles and popularity, up close and personal. They had gotten used to their platform and the feeling of exclusivity they enjoyed as "the twelve," having been chosen from the hundreds of disciples who also followed Jesus. As they entertained thoughts of grandeur and the notion of running the entire nation at Jesus' side, He spoke of leaving. I can feel the panic and fake tears welling up in my eyes as I tried to "persuade" my mom to stay home with us rather than leaving. I wonder what the disciples used to communicate their desire for Jesus to stay. Although scripture does not speak directly to their response, it does tell us about Jesus' reassurances to them. Rather than disappearing without notice, Jesus lets them know that His departure doesn't need to be frightening or filled with agony. His leaving, while uncomfortable, was actually beneficial to them. Even though they would probably be anxious or afraid, Jesus was actually leaving to create something special for them. In fact, Jesus makes His leaving the guarantee of His return. They have watched Him minister and have learned His character and based upon their experience, Jesus guarantees His return.

Finally, Jesus assures them that His leaving is temporary. Although His leaving will be uncomfortable, it will not last forever. When they are tempted to lose hope and to give up, the words of Jesus were a reminder for them, "I'll be back." No matter what the voices in their heads or the voices of the crowds said to them, they had the promise of the Savior, in His words and with His voice, "I'll be back." With that promise, the disciples had to make a decision to be ready to meet Him when He returned. Knowing that He'd return, each of them had a choice as to whether they'd be faithful to their commitment to Him while He was away. Would they decide to move on to something else after He left or would they remain faithful? We have the same decision to make. Jesus has issued His promise along with other promises and we now must determine whether He is worth waiting for.

REFLECTIONS

1. How do you preserve your belief in the return of Jesus Christ?

2. How do you communicate your determination to people who haven't made the same commitment?

MAKE US ONE
| JOHN 16-18

"I have given them the glory you gave me, so they may be one as we are one. I am in them and you are in me. May they experience such perfect unity that the world will know that you sent me and that you love them as much as you love me."

- John 17:22, 23

There's been a great deal of energy expended to demonstrate how unique or different groups of Christ's followers are from one another, when the signature characteristic that Jesus intended for them was unity or togetherness. Jesus' last discourse in the gospels is a passionate conversation with His Father. Many times, I've wondered what the Godhead spoke about during their time together before any other being had been created. I would pay to be a fly on the wall and hear what they discussed with one another and how they shared their hearts with the others. Wouldn't it be amazing to observe how the Godhead interacts? What types of information and wisdom, what mind-blowing revelations would you leave the encounter with? The mere thought is overwhelming. John gives us the gift of eavesdropping on one of those conversations. Here, we see the heart of Jesus laid bare before His Father. Of the many subjects Jesus could have broached, He talks about us.

Jesus lets His concern for us be known and John shares these concerns with us as a reminder of the true nature and values of the Kingdom. Jesus skips a lot of the things that we may be tempted to highlight. Jesus makes no mention of our financial situation; he doesn't pray that God would keep us from trouble but rather keep us through it. Then, Jesus prays that we would be empowered to bring glory to the Father in the same way Jesus does. Again, He doesn't highlight the things that we often prioritize. Jesus says we would bring glory to The Father because we are one. The disciples have already been less than unified. Their concern was for who would be the greatest among them. They wanted to know who would enjoy the most perks as a result of their connection with the Lord. They want to be out front, prominent, noticed by others, and they felt completely justified. They are willing to take each other down to get that "front seat." They wanted to differentiate themselves, so that Jesus would see something special about them and "pick them."

How different is that rat race than our own efforts to make ourselves seem more faithful, more spiritual, and more orthodox than others who are following the same Christ? When we attempt to discredit or expose others who name the name of Christ, who are we really glorifying? Is it our job to expose the true nature of our brothers and sisters in Christ, or is it our job to work toward unity and shared mission?

Jesus seems pretty serious when He declares what will be the sign of His reign in the earth. Unfortunately, it's not orthodoxy, but unity. May God help us to honor Him in the way He intended. May God give us His heart for His people, not based upon our shared practices but based upon our shared Redeemer.

REFLECTIONS

1. What does unity among people with differences look like?

2. How do we create bridges between ourselves and others who are Christian but who worship differently than ourselves?

IF YOU LOVE ME...
| JOHN 19-21

*"A third time he asked him,
'Simon, son of John, do you love me?'*

*Peter was hurt that Jesus asked the question a third time. He
said, 'Lord, you know everything. You know that I love you.'
Jesus said, 'Then feed my sheep.'"*

- John 21:17

It's always interesting to see where Jesus places emphasis. It shows me His core values and demonstrates for me what is truly important. Along with Jesus' concern to empower His disciples for their ministry after His ascension, Jesus has a heart for Peter. The night before Jesus' crucifixion is still heavy on Peter's conscience and though he's present, he still doesn't feel or act like part of the group. He still feels guilty and though Jesus has forgiven him, he still hasn't forgiven himself. So, Jesus takes time to love on Peter to restore his morale and self-confidence before He leaves.

Part of Peter's low self-assurance is affecting his ability to minister to others. In his mind, if he failed Jesus so publicly, how could he stand in front of others to proclaim truth to them? Isn't it interesting how our boldness in representing the Kingdom is often based on our thoughts and feelings about our past or current behavior. Of course, we should be conscientious when we are representing Jesus Christ, but our conceptualization as to the merit of our behavior is traditionally skewed by blurry vision. Put another way, our righteousness is as filthy rags, so we overestimate the role of our behavior in the process. This verse suggests a different criterion for ministry. I'd expect Jesus and Peter to go back through the events of that night and talk through it, together. Maybe they would hug and exchange apology and acceptance. However, that would have fed into the belief that Jesus is looking for us to grovel or to scourge ourselves emotionally to receive forgiveness. So, instead of a long process, Jesus asks a question, "Do you love me?"

"Well, yes, Lord, I love you."

Jesus replies, "Feed my sheep."

Three times, the exchange is made. "Do you love me?"

"Yes, I love you."

"Feed my sheep."

Peter is annoyed because he believes the repeated query is an attempt to question his sincerity. Rather, it seems Jesus is establishing his legitimacy. "Do you love me?"

"Yes."

There it is. Jesus' commissioning of Peter is not based on Peter's history, but anchored in his love. Love is the basis for his establishment in the ministry. Only love. Many people have found ways to make themselves better by legitimizing their work based on things they've gotten right. They feel they belong wherever they are because they've been good. However, when the sinful nature flares up in a way that is evident, they now feel disqualified to serve the Lord and even at His urging, they reject the calling and fade into the shadows of obscurity. This is not what Jesus wanted for Peter. So, He gives him a gift. Now, every time doubt crept into his mind regarding his call, he would have a mental visual and verbal reminder of Jesus' personal call to him to feed Christ's sheep.

For each of the three denials, Peter now has three confirmations. "Yes, I love you." He can rehearse their personal conversation and know that Jesus heard him and accepted him. Peter can now publicly replace the tape and know that Jesus also commissioned him to the ministry at each confession. "Feed my sheep."

The foundation for relationship, the criterion for ministry, is not behavior, it's love. Jesus doesn't go back into any of the old stuff, He establishes that He is looking for love from Peter, though He knows the truth about all Peter has said and done. Now, Peter's motivation for ministry shifts from guilt or absolution to faithfulness. Peter can respond to all detractors and say, with confidence, "I am only doing what Christ told me to do." Anyone with questions can be directed, with confidence, to the One who has charged Peter to minister.

As we end this journey, perhaps Jesus is asking us the same question, "Do you love me?" As we scramble to "get it right" and to overcome our challenges, maybe Jesus wants us to answer the question in our own minds, to pause and recalibrate... "Do you love me?" Rather than scrambling to know what's next, maybe we already know...

"Feed my sheep."

So simple, so profound... so Jesus.

REFLECTIONS

WE'VE BEEN WITH JESUS…
AFTER THE CHALLENGE.

"The disciples saw Jesus do many other miraculous signs in addition to the ones recorded in this book. But these are written so that you may continue to believe that Jesus is the Messiah, the Son of God, and that by believing in him you will have life by the power of his name."

- John 21:17

What a wonderful journey we've had over the past month becoming better acquainted with the Son of God as He is portrayed in the Gospels. It is my hope that you have encountered Jesus in an entirely new way. I am also prayerful that you have found yourself craving time with Jesus and time in His word on a daily basis. In the same way that living organisms need food, water and air on a daily basis in order to remain alive and to have proper nourishment, we must ingest the word of God and be washed and filled by his Spirit on a daily basis.

This is the point where we have to make a decision. We have begun the journey and been filled with new understanding and the rich gems of God's word. Now, the question we must answer for ourselves is, "Will we stop our discovery of Jesus here?" Will we satisfy ourselves with what we've learned thus far and accept it as enough to revitalize us for the days to come? Or will we continually seek God's face and ask for new revelations of God's character and love, every day?

My prayer is that you will continue to chase after new and fresh revelations of Jesus every day. God's desire is to reveal Himself to all his children, not as an abnormal occurrence but through daily interaction. God wants to reenact his daily walks in Eden during our daily time of communion. God wants us to know Him.

As you close this time in the Gospels, I pray that you will consent to daily quiet time with Jesus. God will connect with you in ways you never dreamed of. Thank you so much for joining me on the journey. May we become ever nearer to our Lord and Savior, is my prayer.

REFLECTIONS

1. What time of the day felt most natural for you to spend time in the Word each day?

2. What distractions became obstacles between you and completing your daily challenge readings?

3. What specific place did you gravitate to as you prepared to read each day?

CONNECT WITH
Lola

Looking for a speaker for your next event?
Book Pastor Lola Moore

LET'S STAY CONNECTED!

🐦 **Twitter | @IAMLOLAMOORE**

f **Facebook | PastorLolaMoore**

Website | www.LolaMoore.org

REFLECTIONS

The Gospels Challenge by Lola Moore, M. Div

REFLECTIONS

REFLECTIONS

The Gospels Challenge by Lola Moore, M. Div

REFLECTIONS

REFLECTIONS

The Gospels Challenge by Lola Moore, M. Div

REFLECTIONS

REFLECTIONS

REFLECTIONS

SPIRIT REIGN
PUBLISHING
A Division of Spirit Reign Communications